WALT WHITMAN

IN

WASHINGTON, D.C.

WALT WHITMAN

IN

WASHINGTON, D.C.

THE CIVIL WAR
AND AMERICA'S GREAT POET

GARRETT PECK

Foreword by Martin G. Murray, founder of the Washington Friends of Walt Whitman

THE
History
PRESS

Published by The History Press
Charleston, SC 29403
www.historypress.net

Copyright © 2015 by Garrett Peck
All rights reserved

Front cover, bottom: Campbell Hospital. *Courtesy of the Prints & Photographs Division, Library of Congress.*

First published 2015

ISBN 978.1.54021.385.3

Library of Congress Control Number: 2014959296

Also by Garrett Peck

The Prohibition Hangover: Alcohol in America from Demon Rum to Cult Cabernet (2009)

Prohibition in Washington, D.C.: How Dry We Weren't (2011)

The Potomac River: A History and Guide (2012)

The Smithsonian Castle and the Seneca Quarry (2013)

Capital Beer: A Heady History of Brewing in Washington, D.C. (2014)

CONTENTS

FOREWORD

"This is the city and I am one of the citizens," declared Walt Whitman in his signature poem, "Song of Myself." "Whatever interests the rest interests me." Garrett Peck's engagingly written and amply illustrated guide demonstrates how Whitman immersed himself in Washington's urban fabric while living here from 1863 to 1873. Whitman relished his roles as hospital visitor, loving comrade, federal employee and journalist, all in support of his lifelong vocation as America's poet.

Initially drawn to Washington to nurse his brother George, who was wounded in a Civil War battle, the forty-three-year-old Walt's embrace soon encompassed an army of sick and wounded soldiers housed in Washington's hospitals. Supporting himself by copying reports for the army paymaster, he also began to provide the local and New York presses with compelling descriptions of his hospital visits. These experiences formed the genesis of his wartime poems, a collection entitled *Drum-Taps*. Whitman channeled the Union's grief at President Lincoln's assassination in his powerful elegies, "When Lilacs Last in the Dooryard Bloom'd" and "O Captain! My Captain!" Remaining here after the war, Whitman published a major prose work, *Democratic Vistas*, about the evils of postwar materialism and two more editions of his poetry collection *Leaves of Grass*. He found emotional succor in friendships with soldier Lewis Brown, abolitionists William and Ellen O'Connor, former publisher Charles Eldridge, naturalist John Burroughs, journalist Crosby Stuart Noyes, statesman James Garfield and horsecar conductor Pete Doyle, a former Confederate soldier whom biographers take to be the poet's lover. Government employment was a good fit for the middle-aged poet, and he served as a clerk with the Interior Department's Office of Indian Affairs and the U.S. attorney general. Following a stroke in 1873, Whitman moved permanently to Camden, New Jersey, allowing George to play caregiver to Walt. The poet died on March 26, 1892, and is buried in Camden.

Although living in Washington for a mere decade of his seventy-two years, Whitman devoted nearly a third of his autobiography, *Specimen Days*, to his years in the nation's capital. Peck's emphasis on the city's importance to the poet follows Whitman's lead and is a welcome addition to efforts made by other scholars and enthusiasts. The Washington Friends of Walt Whitman (WFWW), which I formed in 1985, has also attempted to do its part in promoting Walt's D.C. legacy. Two recent events are emblematic. In 2005, we spearheaded "DC Celebrates Whitman: 150 Years of *Leaves of Grass*." Chaired by the incomparable Kim Roberts and presented in partnership with local arts and culture organizations, the citywide celebration featured a wide array of readings by D.C.-based poets influenced by Whitman, tours of local sites associated with the poet and a marathon reading of Whitman's poetry. It culminated with the city's naming a segment of F Street Northwest (in front of the National Portrait Gallery where Whitman nursed wounded soldiers) Walt Whitman Way (see http://washingtonart. com/whitman/walt.html). In 2013, coinciding with the 150th anniversary of Whitman's arrival in D.C., WFWW cosponsored a conference on "Whitman and Melville in DC: The Civil War Years and After" with the Melville Society, George Washington University and Rutgers University–Camden. Conference coordinators Christopher Sten (GWU), Joe Fruscione (GWU), Tyler Hoffman (Rutgers) and I oversaw presentations by more than one hundred leading scholars from around the globe, with keynote addresses by Ed Folsom (University of Iowa), Kenneth Price (University of Nebraska–Lincoln), Elizabeth Renker (Ohio State University) and John Bryant (Hofstra University). The closing banquet at the Arts Club of Washington featured a musical program of Whitman's and Melville's poetry organized by a local bass singer, David Brundage (see http://melvillesociety.org/conferences).

Garrett Peck's study adds further luster to Whitman's fame in D.C. and will surely win Whitman a new generation of admirers to gladden the old poet's heart!

MARTIN G. MURRAY
Founder, Washington Friends of Walt Whitman

ACKNOWLEDGEMENTS

A s I'm fond of saying, no book is written in a vacuum. I am deeply grateful for the assistance from so many people who take their inspiration from Walt Whitman's generous spirit. The poet spent ten crucial years in Washington, D.C., and this city is especially blessed with Walt Whitman admirers. Martin Murray is not only the founder of the Washington Friends of Walt Whitman but also lent his outstanding knowledge of all things Whitman, and he generously wrote the book's foreword. If you visit Peter Doyle's grave at Congressional Cemetery, you can admire the lilac bush that Martin planted there in 2014 in homage to Pete and Walt. Sincere thanks go as well to Sherwood Smith, another Whitman friend whose kindness rivals Walt's.

Archivists and librarians are stewards of our history who open the vaults to researchers like myself. Many of Whitman's records are entrusted to the Library of Congress. Walt would be very proud of our "federal clerks," as am I—especially Dr. Alice Birney, Dr. Barbara Bair and Chris Copetas, who helped guide my research and answered my many questions. Jeff Bridgers in the Prints & Photographs Division has assisted me with many images over the years in numerous books.

Librarians are modern-day superheroes. Jerry McCoy of MLK Library's Washingtoniana room somehow makes his way into most of my books thanks to his inquisitive mind and incredible insight into all things Washington. John Muller piqued my curiosity of the friendship between William Swinton and Mark Twain. Laura Barry at the Historical Society of Washington, D.C., is one of the most adept research assistants I've had the privilege of working with. And the staff at Arlington Central Library patiently dealt with my endless interlibrary loan requests.

Washington is fortunate to have museums that preserve our legacies for future generations. Melissa Kroning and Eleanor Harvey have the privilege of working for the Smithsonian in the old Patent Office, where both Clara Barton and Walt Whitman worked, and both pointed out crucial Civil War material. Susan Rosenvold, the first director of the Clara Barton's Missing Soldiers Office, showed me the museum long before it opened, and Sara Florini provided a personal tour of the space afterward. Terry Reimer of the National Museum of Civil War Medicine shared her extensive knowledge of Civil War–era hospitals. Steve Livengood of the U.S. Capitol Historical Society first raised the question of whether Clara and Walt ever met—and answered it with a painting.

Finally, my sincere gratitude to Kenny Allen for once again providing a superb map and to my editor at The History Press, J. Banks Smither, for championing this project, as well as Katie Parry, Sarah Falter and Julia Turner for their help in bringing Walt Whitman to the public.

Thank you all!

INTRODUCTION

An oversized, slow-moving man ambled into the wards of the Armory Square Hospital in Washington, D.C. He was dressed in a red wine–colored suit with a dandyish cravat tied at his neck, and his graying beard, bushy hair and drooping eyelids gave him an eccentric look—and aged him well beyond his forty-three years. He sauntered in, a wide-brimmed hat in his hand that protected his ruddy face and blue eyes; he sometimes even carried a parasol against the hot Washington sun. Over his shoulder was slung a plump haversack. His fingers were ink stained from copying documents at the Army Paymaster Office that morning.

Located on the National Mall, Armory Square was the largest and most professionally run of the Union's Civil War hospitals and was a marvel of cleanliness and modern medicine. Each ward was a whitewashed wooden building; its walls were plastered, and along them, stoves were neatly arranged to provide heat. The sixty beds were arranged in parallel rows on both sides of the ward with the patients' feet pointing toward the center aisle. White curtains were pulled up over the beds; these could be lowered for privacy and to protect against mosquitoes. Pine branches were hung from the ceiling to freshen the air.

The beds were filled with the recuperating bodies of Union and sometimes Confederate soldiers. The majority of the men were sick, but many were wounded. Some were broken and would soon die. The hospital ward was the soldiers' home, often for months. The more ambulatory men played checkers or chess; others smoked pipes.

The nurses and stewards recognized the gray-bearded man and greeted him with a smile while they continued their rounds. The man came to look after the young soldiers, most of them teenagers, the eldest only in their early twenties. He greeted the soldiers quietly with a simple "Howdy" or "How are you, my boy?" He stopped by every bed and gently chatted with the wounded, sick and dying, paying attention to every soldier, discreetly asking if there was anything they needed. From his leather haversack, he pulled out writing paper and envelopes, jelly, tobacco, fruit, sometimes a bit of money and any special items that a soldier had requested on an earlier visit. He spent far more time listening than speaking, writing down in a small notebook anything that a soldier needed.

The graying man was Walt Whitman.

More than 600,000 people died during the Civil War—and hundreds of thousands more were injured and maimed. Walt's compassion for the sick and wounded stemmed from his deep wellspring of empathy for others. It was this empathy that made so many people fall in love with him. He connected with people, and he listened without judging. He took care of their needs, whether those were a glass of milk, a letter home or just to have a friend sit beside them while their lives ebbed away.

Far from being the slacker and layabout that some have thought, Whitman was an ambitious writer, one who aimed to be America's foremost poet. He showed a great deal of fortitude, publishing his signature poetry book, *Leaves of Grass*, in seven editions between 1855 and 1891. Only three of those editions had a publisher (1860, 1881, 1891). The others he self-published. Walt Whitman is regarded as the poet laureate of the Civil War and, in fact, one of the greatest poets in American history.

For many, their first Walt Whitman reference is the poetic inspiration in the 1989 movie *Dead Poets' Society*. People vividly remember the end of the film, when Ethan Hawke stands on a desk and movingly shouts out, "O Captain! My Captain!" as Robin Williams departs.

When people asked why I was writing this book, I explained that Whitman lived in Washington, D.C., for ten years. "He did?!" was the near-universal response. They knew he served as a hospital volunteer during the Civil War but not that he remained in Washington and took a job as a federal clerk or that he wrote his Civil War poetry book *Drum-Taps* as a Washington resident. Another overlooked fact is that Whitman's partner, Peter Doyle, was in Ford's Theatre and witnessed the tragedy of President Abraham Lincoln's assassination.

Whitman first journeyed to the city in December 1862 to help his wounded brother George after the Battle of Fredericksburg. Ten years later, in January 1873, Walt suffered a stroke that eventually forced him to move into that same brother's home in New Jersey; it was now George's turn to help the stricken poet.

The weekend of Labor Day 2014, I came down with appendicitis and ended up in the hospital, undergoing the knife a few hours after I arrived. The brilliance of modern medicine meant that I received just three tiny laparoscopic incisions before being released the next morning. Modern technology was also a wonder: I had my iPhone with me, texting my parents and updating Facebook until nearly the moment the anesthesiologist put the mask over my face and said, "Breathe." But the most important part was having a friend, Koset Surakomol, who came by the hospital and served as my patient advocate.

This is what Walt Whitman did. He was neither a nurse nor a wound-dresser but more like a one-man United Services Organization, a patient advocate long before the term was invented. He provided an absolutely vital service: friendship in the face of adversity, a morale boost to any soldier facing the worst. As he described in his 1876 book *Memoranda During the War*, "I am merely a friend visiting the Hospitals occasionally to cheer the wounded and sick."[1]

My experience in the hospital was easy compared to those who fought in the Civil War. True, surgeons then had the benefit of anesthesia to render their patients unconscious prior to surgery. But surgery was often amputations, and the recovery time wasn't measured in days or weeks but in months. There were no antibiotics. Thousands of soldiers died from infections.

And though the hospitals were full of good doctors and nurses, the soldiers were very much alone, being separated from their friends and military units, finding themselves in a strange hospital bed in a strange city. The Civil War was the first time away from home for many of these young men—and certainly the biggest adventure any of them would face.

The Civil War affected everyone—not just the soldiers doing the fighting. In these pages you'll read about people like Clara Barton and Louisa May Alcott, as well as Walt Whitman, people who never put on a uniform but, as civilians, lent great support to the war effort. These people made a real difference to the soldiers.

Whitman's presence is remembered in Washington long after he left the city in 1873. He is considered one of the fathers of the district's gay community—and he was, appropriately, a federal employee. To this day, his name—along with that of Dr. Mary Walker, a female surgeon during

The portion of F Street Northwest along the south front of the Smithsonian American Art Museum is designated as Walt Whitman Way. *Garrett Peck.*

the Civil War—adorns the Whitman-Walker Clinic, a facility that has long addressed HIV/AIDS. Other landmarks are found on the city's landscape. Walt Whitman Way is the designated portion of F Street Northwest in front of the Smithsonian American Art Museum (the old Patent Office where Whitman briefly worked).

Coming out of the north entrance of the Dupont Circle Metro station, you'll see part of Whitman's poem "The Wound-Dresser" carved into the giant stone circle that surrounds the entrance:

> *Thus in silence, in dreams' projections,*
> *Returning, resuming, I thread my way through the hospitals;*
> *The hurt and wounded I pacify with soothing hand,*
> *I sit by the restless all the dark night—some are so young;*
> *Some suffer so much—I recall the experience sweet and sad…*

The poem was carved into the station entrance in 2007. It echoes the AIDS crisis of the 1980s and 1990s, when thousands of gay men were dying

The north entrance to the Dupont Metro station quotes Whitman's poem "The Wound-Dresser." *Garrett Peck.*

of the disease. Another Whitman poem is quoted at the Archives–Navy Memorial Metro station, his "Prayer of Columbus." Two more are carved in pink granite in Freedom Plaza, one from 1855, the other from 1888. In the Mount Pleasant neighborhood, there is a firebox converted into street art showing Civil War casualties arriving at Mount Pleasant Hospital. The back quotes Whitman's poem "Dirge for Two Veterans."

Walt Whitman is widely accepted today as being gay (he began his longest romantic relationship, with Peter Doyle, while cruising on a streetcar in early 1865), yet the word *homosexual* wasn't first used in print until 1892, the year of his death. In Whitman's lifetime, "gay" simply meant happy. The cultural vocabulary of today's LGBT community didn't exist in Whitman's time to describe same-sex attraction and love.

Whitman lived at six different sites around the city, and none of them survives. However, his places of employment are largely intact. The Washington of Whitman's day gave way to redevelopment in the twentieth century, and with it, many historical structures and neighborhoods were demolished for downtown office buildings.

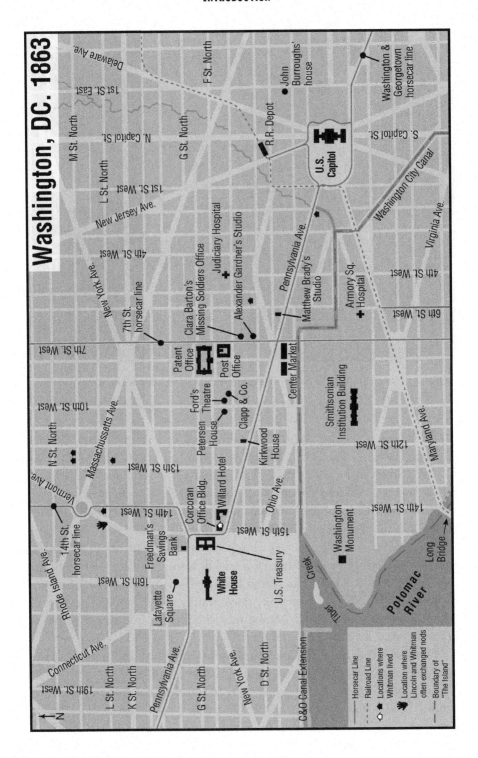

Washington, DC. 1863

Delaware Ave.
F St. North
John Burroughs' house
Washington & Georgetown horsecar line
1st St. East
M St. North
R.R. Depot
N. Capitol St.
G St. North
S. Capitol St.
L St. North
1st St. West
U.S. Capitol
New Jersey Ave.
Washington City Canal
4th St. West
Judiciary Hospital
Pennsylvania Ave.
Virginia Ave.
New York Ave.
Clara Barton's Missing Soldiers Office
Alexander Gardner's Studio
Matthew Brady's Studio
Armory Sq. Hospital
4th St. West
7th St. horsecar line
6th St. West
7th St. West
Patent Office
Post Office
Center Market
Smithsonian Institution Building
10th St. West
Ford's Theatre
Clapp & Co.
N St. North
Massachussetts Ave.
Petersen House
Kirkwood House
12th St. West
Maryland Ave.
Vermont Ave.
13th St. West
Willard Hotel
Corcoran Office Bldg.
Ohio Ave.
14th St. West
14th St. horsecar line
Freedman's Savings Bank
14th St. West
15th St. West
Washington Monument
14th St. West
Rhode Island Ave.
Lafayette Square
White House
U.S. Treasury
Creek
Long Bridge
Connecticut Ave.
16th St. West
Tiber
Potomac River
19th St. West
L St. North
K St. North
Pennsylvania Ave.
G St. North
New York Ave.
D St. North
C&O Canal Extension

Horsecar Line
Railroad Line
Locations where Whitman lived
Location where Lincoln and Whitman often exchanged nods
Boundary of "The Island"

N

Like most cities at the time, Washington had a number of daily newspapers that were the primary sources of public information. During Whitman's time, the paper of record was the *Daily National Intelligencer*, which folded in 1869. The *Evening Star*, published starting in 1852, took over the mantle as the leading newspaper in the city. But there were others as well, such as the *Chronicle* and the *Critic-Record*. I have overwhelmingly relied on primary material.

Many people wrote recollections of Walt Whitman, and these are excellent primary sources, though at times problematic. Memory is sometimes tarnished with time, but more often, it grows more lustrous as we romanticize the past. Whitman's friend John Swinton penned an 1876 letter to the *New York Herald* that was glorious in recollection but somewhat dim on details. More than ten years after the Civil War, he described Walt as carrying a "little basket" through the hospitals when, in fact, it was a leather haversack. He thought Walt supported the wounded from the Peninsula Campaign (more than half a year before Walt arrived in Washington). Swinton's language is effusive praise, and every wounded soldier offers a chorus of love for the saintly Whitman. It's a bit over the top, although not uncommon for people who knew Walt.[2]

Whitman himself was a prolific writer, and much of his writing is preserved and even digitized, such as that on the Whitman Archive (www. whitmanarchive.org). Whitman himself is the primary source for this book, especially his hundreds of letters, his book *Memoranda During the War* (1876) and his dozens of unpublished notebooks. He also wrote as a freelance correspondent for the *New York Times* and *Brooklyn Daily Eagle* during the Civil War.

In the Library of Congress today are tens of thousands of Walt Whitman objects that are part of the Charles E. Feinberg and Thomas B. Harned collections, as well as related manuscript collections. Since 1990, Dr. Alice Birney has had stewardship of these Whitman collections, serving as literary historian of the Manuscript Division. When I asked what Whitman meant to her, she explained how she had read stanzas of "When Lilacs Last in the Dooryard Bloom'd" at her husband's funeral. "It felt just right," she said. Dr. Barbara Bair, the division's nineteenth-century historian, said of Whitman, "He's one of the greatest literary figures of the nineteenth century."

In his great poem "Crossing Brooklyn Ferry," Whitman offered a glimpse of the eternal, the continuity between generations, even far removed: "The men and women I saw were all near to me; / Others the same—others who look back on me because I look'd forward to them,…What is it, then, between us? / What is the count of the scores or hundreds of years between us? / Whatever it is, it avails not—distance avails not, and place avails not." In looking back to Walt, we find him reaching forward to us with a gentle hand and a warm smile.

Chapter 1

WALT WHITMAN, AN AMERICAN

Walter Whitman was born on May 31, 1819, on Long Island, New York. He was the second of nine children to Walter Whitman Sr. and Louisa Van Velsor Whitman (eight children lived to see adulthood). The family had lived on Long Island for two centuries. Walt's parents moved the family to Brooklyn when he was a child.

The Whitmans were a working-class family. Walt Sr. was an artisan and construction worker who dabbled in real estate development. Louisa was a homemaker who wrestled with the daily life of feeding a small army of people and coping with the family's never-ending drama: one son would go insane, another died of tuberculosis (or, more likely, syphilis) and another was born mentally disabled. The Whitmans were Quakers, though they weren't religious. Walt was hardly a churchgoer.

Walt received a grade school education and then learned the printing trade as a teenager. He went on to become a journalist, writing for the *Brooklyn Daily Eagle* and the *Freeman*. After the *Freeman* folded in 1848, Whitman journeyed to New Orleans, where he witnessed the evils of slavery firsthand. In his career path, Walt learned not only how to write well but also how to print and typeset. This came in handy when he self-published his first volume of poetry, *Leaves of Grass*, as he was intimately involved in the printing of each page.

Walt was a large man, six feet tall and burly. He would steadily gain weight until he was on the cusp of two hundred pounds on the eve of the Civil War. His beard began graying in his twenties, and his hair soon followed.

He looked prematurely aged, like a vigorous older man. Whitman never married. He was, to use a euphemism, a confirmed bachelor.

Despite his humble origins and lack of higher education, Walt was drawn to literature and was a voracious reader. He especially loved Shakespeare. Whitman came in touch with the ideas of Ralph Waldo Emerson, one of the leading American thinkers of the nineteenth century. "I was simmering, simmering, simmering; Emerson brought me to a boil," Whitman said.[3] The transcendentalist Emerson was a mentor to a generation of poets and writers. Whitman first heard Emerson speak in 1842, but it would be more than a decade before Walt finally responded to the muse. It took him years to find his own voice. And find it he did.

While Henry David Thoreau, an Emerson disciple, abolitionist and author of *Walden*, worshipped nature, Whitman was unapologetically an urban creature, a Brooklynite who spent most of his life in cities, close to the bustle of factories, ports and railroads and always close to the "roughs" (as he called them), the working-class men toward whom he gravitated. Whitman's friend John Burroughs described him thus: "Fond of cities, he has gone persistently into all their haunts and by-places, not as a modern missionary and reformer, but as a student and lover of men, finding beneath all forms of vice and degradation the same old delicious, yearning creatures, after all."[4]

Whitman rejected the conceit of dualism, popular since René Descartes in the seventeenth century, that the body was a cage for the soul or that the body was itself sinful while the soul was pure. Burroughs observed how Walt referred to the body in his poetry: "Nothing is more intoxicating, nothing more sacred than the Body; he often capitalizes the word, as is done with the name of the Deity."[5]

Walt struck many as a quiet slacker, but in fact, he was keenly ambitious. He wanted to be regarded as America's greatest poet. Responding to Emerson's call for a distinctly American voice in literature, Whitman set out to reinvent poetry.

LEAVES OF GRASS

In July 1855, Whitman self-published his poetry book *Leaves of Grass*, which included his famous poem "Song of Myself." He printed eight hundred copies of the book, which initially had twelve poems. He would continually revise and add to the poetry collection throughout his life, publishing altogether seven editions of *Leaves of Grass*. Whitman's poetry was celebratory—and it was also erotic, which made him both controversial and popular in an era of Victorian prudery. Some considered Whitman's work obscene.

The author image that accompanied *Leaves of Grass* showed a casual Whitman wearing working-class clothing, the shirt open at the collar accentuating his copious chest hair. His left hand rested in his baggy pants pocket, his right hand assertively on his hip. His graying hair and beard were closely cropped, and a hat was

Walt Whitman's image printed in the 1855 edition of *Leaves of Grass*. *Library of Congress*.

jauntily perched on his head. The image listed the author's name but also showed off his ambition: "Walt Whitman, An American." This photo shows a man who was carefully crafting his image. He would cultivate that image—that of a vigorous working-class man, a mechanic, "one of the roughs, a Kosmos"—through the Civil War era.

Whitman's father died on July 11, 1855—a week after *Leaves of Grass* was published. Walt's mother, Louisa, became the center of the family. Though Walt was the second-oldest child, he was far from able to support the family financially, but she never seemed to criticize her artistic son for being a dreamer. He was especially close to his mother, and Walt was her favorite child. Whitman loved his mother and put her on a pedestal. Most of Whitman's family ignored *Leaves of Grass*, other than his brother Jeff, who was Walt's closest brother.

Whitman had little formal education and was no college graduate; nor was he of the academy. Free of rules but not of democracy or equality, Whitman invented a free verse form of poetry. He ignored metering and rhyming and wrote in his own cadence and in the common tongue of the working class, often using the slang of the New York docks and streets. "I sound my barbaric yawp over the roofs of the world," he wrote in "Song of Myself." He described language as having "its bases broad and low, close to the ground."[6] He deliberately positioned himself as the antithesis of a man of letters, though he relished reading Shakespeare and going to the opera.

The "barbaric yawp" became so well known that it was also subject to ridicule. The gossipy *Critic-Record* teased in 1871: "Walt Whitman is yawping around Long Island with dyspepsia."[7]

Walt was fiercely egalitarian. He was a democratic poet who demanded equality of the sexes (though he would later have reservations about suffrage for both blacks and women). He didn't shirk from sexuality in his poetry. Yet the working-class men whom Whitman hung around probably had no idea that Whitman was a poet—nor would they likely have understood his poetry had they read it.

William Douglas O'Connor, Walt's most devout defender, characterized Whitman's poetry: "Here, in its grandest, freest use, is the English language, from its lowest compass to the top of the key; from the powerful, rank idiom of the streets and fields, to the last subtlety of academic speech—ample, various, telling, luxuriant, pictorial, final, conquering."[8] Long before modern psychology, Whitman's poetry introduced an intense self-examination. "Song of Myself" opens: "I celebrate myself and sing myself." But who was the "I" of whom he wrote? Whitman often used the first person, but he didn't necessarily mean "I, Walt Whitman." The narrator often changed identities. His 1865 poem "The Wound-Dresser" uses the first person, yet Walt never served as a nurse, though he certainly witnessed hospital stewards and nurses change countless bandages.

Whitman could be full of obfuscations. His worldview was keenly informed by Emerson and transcendentalism, though he would deny it later in life. Literary critic Harold Bloom realized this: "The largest puzzle about the continuing reception of Whitman's poetry is the still prevalent notion that we ought to take him at his word, whether about his self (or selves) or about his art. No other poet insists so vehemently and so continuously that he will tell us all, and tell us all without artifice, and yet tells us so little, and so cunningly."[9] Historian Clara Barrus put it even more succinctly: "One is struck with the poet's many-sidedness."[10]

Knowing that Emerson might be interested in his distinctly American poetry, Whitman sent him a copy of the first edition of *Leaves of Grass*. Emerson wrote back an effusive letter. "I find it the most extraordinary piece of wit and wisdom America has yet contributed," he gushed. "I greet you at the beginning of a great career, which yet must have had a long foreground somewhere, for such a start." Whitman used this letter—without Emerson's permission—to promote the second edition of *Leaves of Grass* (1856), which added twenty new poems. He even printed the phrase "I greet you at the beginning of a great career" in gold on the book's spine. It earned mixed reviews and generated controversy for the use of Emerson's letter.[11]

"The United States themselves are essentially the greatest poem," Whitman wrote in the essay that prefaced the 1855 edition of *Leaves of Grass*, and he hoped he would be the national poet, an ambitious but naïve goal. Walt believed his poetry to be "the new American Bible."

Whitman had a knack for self-promotion. He published anonymous reviews to praise his poetry in the hope of widening his audience. He was constantly on the lookout for literary reviews—even if he had to write them himself. If there is a blemish to Whitman's character, it was this need to blow his own horn—often anonymously—for the sheer sake of drawing attention to his work. He was a trendsetter for self-promotion.

Along with Emily Dickenson, Walt Whitman is considered America's greatest nineteenth-century poet. The reclusive Dickenson was repulsed by the very thought of publishing her work and remained out of the public's eye until after her death whereas Whitman craved attention and recognition. He wished to be regarded as America's poet, and by the end of his life, when he was infirm and wracked by poor health, he would be.

QUICKSAND YEARS

Whitman had tried his hand at two editions of poetry, but his writing wasn't a commercial success. He earned few royalties and couldn't support himself or his extended family. He returned to journalism, editing the *Brooklyn Daily Times* for two years (1857–59), and then that, too, petered out. He began a relationship with Fred Vaughan, a stage driver, an affair that inspired the homoerotic "Calamus" poems. He worked only occasionally, preferring the life of an idler, riding the omnibuses for free, picking up men, visiting injured stage drivers in the hospitals and drinking beer at Pfaff's with the fellow bohemians of his literary circle.

Author, critic and playwright William Dean Howells, later an editor at *Atlantic Monthly*, was introduced to Whitman at Pfaff's for the first time in 1860. Howells recalled the moment: "I remember how he leaned back in his chair, and reached out his great hand to me, as if he were going to give it to me for good and all. He had a fine head, with a cloud of Jovian hair upon it, and a branching beard and mustache, and gentle eyes that looked most kindly into mine, and seemed to wish the liking which I instantly gave him, though we hardly passed a word." Whitman surprised him. "The apostle of the rough, the uncouth, was the gentlest person; his barbaric yawp, translated into the terms of social encounter, was an address of singular quiet, delivered in a voice of winning and endearing friendliness."[12] Likewise, novelist John Trowbridge, upon first meeting Whitman, remembered: "I found him the quietest of men."[13]

Whitman was often quiet—except when the subject of his poetry came up. He loved when people discussed his art. He was a better listener than talker, a skill that would serve him well in hundreds of hospital visits during the Civil War. His personality was directed inward, though like many introverts he could be gregarious among intimate friends.

Then came unexpected news: the Boston publishing firm of William Wilde Thayer and Charles Eldridge approached Whitman about publishing his third edition of *Leaves of Grass*. Walt jumped at the chance, moving to Boston for several months in early 1860 to oversee the printing. It was an ambitious expansion, coming in at 456 pages, and included the sexually suggestive "Calamus" and "Enfans d'Adam" poems. Emerson visited Whitman in Boston and tried politely to get Whitman to remove some of the sex, but Walt wouldn't budge. The edition was met by a great deal of criticism, mostly stemming from the belief that its overt sexuality was inappropriate for women. Some called for his poems to be censored for their indecency. That said, the language was hardly pornographic.

It is difficult to fathom Whitman's sexuality. He wrote for posterity, always with an eye on his public image, and he never directly admitted his same-sex attractions. Yet it is also clear, despite some poetry that includes women's sexuality, that Whitman was gay. The vocabulary we have today didn't exist in his time. Whitman never had to "come out." There was little doubt of Whitman's sexual orientation with the "Calamus" poems in the third edition of *Leaves of Grass*. (Calamus is a phallic-shaped flower, and the poems in this section were erotic and highly suggestive of male-male encounters.) And his letters to Peter Doyle, Alonzo Bush and many others make it quite clear that Whitman was attracted to young, working-class men.

Many of the poems in the 1860 edition celebrated the Union. Whitman remained naïvely ambitious, believing that his poems would create cohesiveness between Americans and thus heal the sectional split that would lead to the Civil War. Some of his devotees considered him to be a prophet, though his poetry never did give rise to a religion. He was also naïve in hoping that his poetry would find a mass following. The problem—then as now—was that Americans really weren't poetry readers.

The third edition of *Leaves of Grass* sold well and went through several printings, but it wasn't widely absorbed. The country was splintered along sectional lines as abolitionism became a political force in the North and the South fiercely defended its "peculiar institution" of slavery. The pending crisis of the Civil War was just over the horizon. Whitman's poetic talk about national unity fell on deaf ears.

WHITMAN AND THE CIVIL WAR

Many scholars have thought of the 1860 to 1862 period, after he published the third edition of *Leaves of Grass*, as Whitman's "lost years." Whitman referred to this time as his "quicksand years." The public's appetite for novels and poetry was eclipsed by the need for daily news of the war. Whitman may have been depressed in the years after his latest publication failed to meet his ambitions or heal the nation. The pending crisis between the states was at hand.[14]

With the election of Abraham Lincoln to the presidency in 1860, the Southern states began seceding from the Union, starting with South Carolina. The economy spiraled downward in the crisis. Walt's publisher Thayer & Eldridge went out of business. Eldridge decamped for Washington to the U.S. Army Paymaster Office.

On February 19, 1861, Whitman first glimpsed Abraham Lincoln at Astor Place as Lincoln journeyed to Washington for the inauguration. By this point, seven Southern states had seceded, and more would follow. A large crowd gathered to see the president and watched him in utter silence. Walt recorded his impressions of the man: "The figure, the look, the gait, are distinctly impres'd upon me yet; the unusual and uncouth height, the dress of complete black, the stovepipe hat push'd back on the head, the dark-brown complexion, the seam'd and wrinkled yet canny-looking face, the black, bushy head of hair, the disproportionately long neck, and the hands held behind as he stood observing the people. All was comparative and ominous silence."[15] New York City was no friend to Lincoln—it was a Democratic stronghold that didn't vote for the Republican president—but Whitman was already intrigued.

On April 12, Confederate forces opened fire on Fort Sumter in Charleston Harbor, the opening salvo of the four-year Civil War. The Union garrison surrendered two days later. On April 15, Lincoln called for seventy-five thousand volunteers to put down the insurrection. Virginia immediately began the process of secession, its voters ratifying the decision on May 23. The next day, the Union army crossed the Potomac River to secure Alexandria, Virginia, and the commanding hills above the port city in order to protect the nation's capital.

Walt was nearly forty-two when the Civil War broke out, too old to enlist. Given his pacifist tendencies, it is unthinkable that he would serve in the military. However, his younger brother George enlisted in the Thirteenth New York State Militia for three months and then in the Fifty-first New York Infantry Regiment. George served for the duration of the war, rising from private to colonel. Another brother, Jeff, started a family and began his career as a waterworks engineer. He paid $400 for a substitute in lieu of military service. Jeff became a key fundraiser for Walt's hospital visits.

Whitman was an unapologetic Unionist who stood against slavery. As the North martialed its forces in 1861, Whitman published a poem, "Beat! Beat! Drums!," that reflected the anxious war fever as the volunteer regiments assembled and shipped out to Washington, D.C. It become one of Whitman's best-known and most widely distributed poems. He later included it in *Drum-Taps* (1865).

An 1862 carte de visite of Walt Whitman, taken by Matthew Brady in New York before Whitman came to Washington. *Library of Congress.*

Beat! beat! drums!—blow! bugles! blow!
Though the windows—though the doors—burst like a ruthless force,
Into the solemn church, and scatter the congregation,
Into the school where the scholar is studying;
Leave not the bridegroom quiet—no happiness must he have now with
*   his bride,*
Nor the peaceful farmer any peace, ploughing his field or gathering his grain,
So fierce you whirr and pound you drums—so shrill you bugles blow.

The martial nature of his poetry would change considerably as the war progressed and Walt witnessed firsthand the immense human suffering and death.

Whitman dabbled in journalism during the early years of the Civil War. He continued visiting injured stage drivers at New York hospitals. The wards began to fill with sick and wounded Union soldiers, most of them teenagers or in their early twenties, the type of men Whitman gravitated toward. From Brooklyn, he frequently wrote to his brother George and kept tabs on the progress of the war through the newspapers.

THE BATTLE OF FREDERICKSBURG

Fredericksburg, Virginia, was one of the most fought-over cities in the Civil War. The town was a strategic spot for the Confederacy to defend, as it lay fifty miles south of Washington, D.C.—and halfway to Richmond, the Confederate capital. The Rappahannock River protected the town like a moat, and just to the south was a long ridge known as Marye's Heights. Here Confederate general Robert E. Lee emplaced his Army of Northern Virginia as the Union Army of the Potomac once more marched on Richmond in December 1862.

The Union commander at the time, General Ambrose Burnside, attacked Lee at Fredericksburg. His engineers brought up pontoons, and early on the morning of December 11, they began building temporary bridges over the Rappahannock. At daybreak, Confederate snipers opened fire, inflicting many casualties. The Federals responded with a massive artillery barrage that heavily damaged the town. Burnside pushed troops into Fredericksburg to root out the snipers. Engineers completed the bridges, and the Union army crossed the river in force.

Burnside didn't attack until December 13, giving Lee two more days to concentrate his army. Lee's position was impregnable. Along Marye's

Heights was a stone wall that stood as a ready-made defensive line, and he had positioned dozens of artillery batteries atop the ridge. To his front were a vast open field and a canal that Union forces would have to cross before reaching the Confederate lines. It was a perfect killing ground.

After failing to turn the Confederate right flank, Burnside ordered a frontal assault on Lee's position. The attack was suicidal. The Union army assaulted in wave after wave, and the Confederates slaughtered them. Lieutenant George Whitman was in one of those waves, and afterward, he wrote to his brother Jeff, describing the futile frontal attacks that killed and wounded thousands of men:

> *It was a mighty warm place we were into when I was hit, as the Rebs had a battery planted right in front of us and not more than 1000 yards distance, and they poured grape and canister into us like the very devil. You see we had to advance over a level plane and their batteries being on high ground and they being behind breastworks we had no chance at them, while they could take as deliberate aim as a fellow would at a chicken, the range was so short, that they threw percussion shells into our ranks, that would drop at our feet and explode killing and wounded[.] Three or four every pop. It was a piece of one of that kind of varmints that struck me in the jaw, the shell burst right at my feet so I think that I got off pretty luckey* [sic].[16]

Alfred Waugh sketched this dramatic night march of Union troops as Fredericksburg burns on December 11, 1863, two days before the Union defeat. *Library of Congress.*

George wrote to his mother, Louisa: "I had the side of my jaw slightly scraped with a peice [*sic*] of shell which burst at my feet."[17] It was a flesh wound, but nonetheless, his name was printed in the list of casualties in the newspapers.

The Battle of Fredericksburg was one of the most lopsided, demoralizing defeats for the Army of the Potomac. More than 12,600 Union soldiers were casualties, and nothing had been gained. Witnessing the awful butchery of the Union troops, General Lee remarked, "It is well that war is so terrible, or we should grow too fond of it." Union troops, remembering the slaughter seven months later at Gettysburg, shouted after repelling Pickett's Charge: "Fredericksburg!"

Walt Visits the Army

On December 16, 1862, Whitman's family read the news that every family with a son in the military must dread. George appeared in the *New York Herald* in a list of wounded after the Battle of Fredericksburg. The listing misspelled George's name: "First Lieutenant G.W. Whitmore, Company D," but the company and regiment were correct, so it could only be George. The *New York Times* correctly listed George the following day: "Lieut. Whitman, Co. E, 51st New York—cheek." Not that Walt saw it: he had packed his bag and departed for Washington within hours after seeing his brother's name in the *Herald*.

Walt was pickpocketed in Philadelphia when he switched trains. His friend and publisher Charles Eldridge made the sly remark, "Any pickpocket who failed to avail himself of such an opportunity as Walt offered, with his loose baggy trousers, and no suspenders, would have been a disgrace to his profession."[18] Whitman arrived in Washington without a penny. He searched the hospitals for two days, but he couldn't find George.

The war had brought many people to Washington, including Eldridge and William Douglas O'Connor. In 1860, Eldridge had published both the third edition of *Leaves of Grass* and O'Connor's antislavery novel, *Harrington: A Story of True Love*. The three men had become friends in Boston. Walt looked up his two friends, who immediately provided him with some cash. He wanted to venture to the Union army camp at Falmouth, Virginia, to see if George might be there. Eldridge secured a pass to the front from his boss, Major Lyman Hapgood, at the Army Paymaster Office.

Walt traveled from Washington by packet steamer to Aquia Landing and then took a short military railroad ride to Falmouth, where he quickly found the Fifty-first New York's camp—and George, who was very much in one piece. "When I found dear brother George, and found that he was alive and well, O you may imagine how trifling all my little cares and difficulties seemed—they vanished into nothing," Walt wrote to his mother on December 29. "George was wounded by a shell, a gash in the cheek—you could stick a splint through into the mouth, but it has healed up without difficulty already."

Walt was at the Union army camp at Falmouth, opposite Fredericksburg, for nine days, staying in his brother's tent with the other officers of George's regiment. He spent Christmas in the camp and began writing his first poems about the war in his notebook. Walt also experienced firsthand the conditions that the army lived in, as he wrote to his mother:

> *And now that I have lived for eight or nine days amid such scenes as the camps furnish, and had a practical part in it all, and realize the way that hundreds of thousands of good men are now living, and have had to live for a year or more, not only without any of the comforts, but with death and sickness and hard marching and hard fighting, (and no success at that,) for their continual experience—really nothing we call trouble seems worth talking about. One of the first things that met my eyes in camp, was a heap of feet, arms, legs, &c. under a tree in front a hospital, the Lacy house.*[19]

The grand Lacy House mansion, better known today as Chatham Manor, was a Union army field hospital that overlooked the Rappahannock. This was Walt's first visit to such a place, and he must have thought it butchery, though in fact the field hospitals were well organized and designed to operate on soldiers before infections set in. Clara Barton was working in the Lacy

House at the same time. Clara and Walt's paths may have crossed there, yet neither recorded meeting the other.

Walt returned to Washington on December 28, accompanying the sick and wounded soldiers bound for hospitals and assisting them as he could. "On the boat I had my hands full. One poor fellow died going up," he recalled.[20] Walt decided not to return to Brooklyn but to stay in Washington. In helping the wounded soldiers, Walt realized that he could contribute to the war effort and end his "New York stagnation," as he called it.[21]

Without George Whitman's service in the Union army, Walt would not have experienced the Civil War like he did. In many ways, the war made Whitman. It gave him a purpose. It gave him focus. It gave him a grand opportunity to serve in the cause of humanity—and without picking up a rifle. Walt never saw the chaos of a battle—only the carnage and human wreckage afterward. The war would be the central event of his life.

Chapter 2

THE CITY OF ARMY WAGONS

W hitman had no intention of staying in Washington when he arrived in December 1862. So why did he end up making the city his home for the next ten years? It seemed to be a spontaneous decision. He concluded a December 29 letter to his mother: "I will stay here for the present, at any rate long enough to see if I can get any employment at any thing, and shall write what luck I have."[22]

By the time Whitman arrived in Washington, the capital had been transformed into an armed camp by twenty months of war. Sixty-eight forts encircled the city, protecting it against Confederate attack. A steady flow of steamships brought the wounded from the Virginia battlefields to the hospitals. The city was turned into a giant hospital ward with dozens of facilities scattered about. At any given time, there were thousands of wounded soldiers in the city. And it was the desperate plight of these young men that convinced Whitman to remain in Washington and to help wherever he could.

WASHINGTON AT WAR

The city of Washington wasn't much to look at. It had a handful of well-intentioned but incomplete public buildings—above all, the unfinished U.S. Capitol, its incomplete cast-iron dome shrouded in scaffolding. Whitman

The incomplete U.S. Capitol and Trinity Episcopal Church during the early days of the Civil War. *Library of Congress.*

marveled at the building. He called it "a vast eggshell, built of iron and glass, this dome."[23] It was completed in 1863, a testament that democracy can thrive even in wartime.

The unfinished stub of the Washington Monument, its construction halted only a third of the way up, poked awkwardly out of a hill overlooking the tidal marshes of the Potomac River. They would be filled in the 1880s, putting the monument a half mile from the river. The grassy area around the monument was pasture for raising cows, and a slaughterhouse stood nearby. The cows raised a huge amount of dust. *Frank Leslie's Illustrated* magazine in 1862 called it the "Beef Depot Monument."

The President's House, also known informally as the White House, was hardly more dignified. The Ellipse was then a horse corral known as the "White Lot." A fish market stood nearby at Fifteenth Street and the Potomac River. The mansion lay near the Potomac flats and the malodorous

Washington City Canal. Bridges crossed the canal to reach Southwest—a neighborhood that everyone called the "Island"—and the distinctly dusty rose-colored Smithsonian Institution Building, set apart from the white sandstone buildings of official Washington.

Then there was the Patent Office, the largest public space in the city and the one site most tourists visited for its unique collection of patent models. The building was downtown, away from the horrible-smelling canal but in the heart of the city's commercial district.

The city's boundaries were the Potomac River to the west, the Eastern Branch (Anacostia River) to the south and east and Boundary Street (now Florida Avenue) to the north. Beyond these was farmland. The original plan for the city that Pierre L'Enfant had designed had yet to be filled in, and there were major gaps between many buildings. Dupont Circle, just a few blocks north of the White House, didn't exist yet.

Much of Washington looked incomplete. The grand avenues were nothing but broad, vacant unpaved boulevards, dusty in drought and muddy messes after it rained. Two decades before Walt Whitman's arrival, English novelist Charles Dickens visited Washington in 1842.

> *It is sometimes called the City of Magnificent Distances, but it might with greater propriety be termed the City of Magnificent Intentions; for it is only on taking a bird's-eye view of it from the top of the Capitol that one can at all comprehend the vast designs of its projector, an aspiring Frenchman. Spacious avenues, that begin in nothing, and lead nowhere; streets, mile long, that only want houses, roads, and inhabitants; public buildings that need but a public to be complete; and ornaments of great thoroughfares, which only lack great thoroughfares to ornament—are its leading features.*[24]

The city changed little in the following years—until the war came. The Civil War transformed Washington from a sleepy City of Magnificent Distances into a crowded citadel and bustling hub.

British novelist Anthony Trollope visited Washington on Christmas Day 1861. The capital's transformation into an armed camp was underway, but Trollope was more concerned with architecture, the broad empty boulevards and the lack of society. He declared the city a failure: "But Washington is but a ragged, unfinished collection of unbuilt broad streets, as to the completion of which there can now, I imagine, be but little hope."[25]

Elisha Hunt Rhodes, a Rhode Island volunteer who served in the Union army for the entire war and kept a lengthy diary of his experience, first arrived

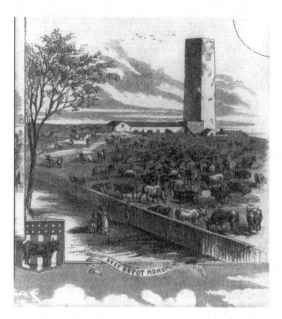

Cattle graze near the incomplete Washington Monument, which the artist dubbed the "Beef Depot Monument." *Library of Congress.*

An 1858 view of the south front of the White House. *Library of Congress.*

in Washington in June 1861 and described what he saw: "Hurrah we are in Washington and what a city! Mud, pigs, geese, Negroes, palaces, shanties everywhere." Some forty thousand former slaves known as "contrabands" found their freedom within this citadel but struggled to find a place to live. They often ended up in shanties.[26]

John Hay, one of President Abraham Lincoln's private secretaries, described for the *New York World* the drunken scene that he found in Washington just before the inauguration. "If one be bitten with the desire of legislation or other fame, Washington is a good place to disillutionise [*sic*] him," he wrote. The clientele of bars and hotels represented "every stage of official eminence and every grade of inebriety. There are generals, and colonels, and majors, and captains, governors, senators, honorable; all chew tobacco; all spit; a good many swear, and not a few make a merit of being able to keep two cocktails in the air at once."[27]

On the other hand, Washington could also be quite exciting. The city was crowded with people coming and going—sutlers, politicians and thousands of soldiers. It became difficult to find a room in a hotel or a boardinghouse. Washington faced a severe housing shortage. More than 200,000 civilians and soldiers crowded into a city that before the war had numbered only 65,000 people.[28] With so many people in town, theaters like Ford's and the National had no problem filling seats. Gamblers could exercise the sporting life at the city's many illegal casinos, and there were plenty of brothels to satisfy any whim. German immigrants opened breweries, beer gardens and saloons to quench the insatiable thirst of civilians and soldiers.

The main source of entertainment was along Pennsylvania Avenue—what most simply referred to as the "Avenue"—along the mile between the Capitol and the White House. Louisa May Alcott described the excitement that she found in the city: "Pennsylvania Avenue, with its bustle, lights, music, and military, made me feel as if I'd crossed the water and landed somewhere in Carnival time."[29] Strolling the Avenue would become one of Whitman's favorite pastimes.

The Willard Hotel was the center of Washington's social life. Shortly before the Civil War began, secret last-minute negotiations were held there to forestall the crisis. Julia Ward Howe composed "Battle Hymn of the Republic" while a guest at the hotel. And novelist Nathaniel Hawthorne stayed at the Willard during a wartime visit to Washington. "This hotel, in fact, may be much more justly called the centre of Washington than either the Capitol, the White House, or the State Department. Everybody may be seen there," he declared. He seemed to enjoy himself more than Trollope had. "You adopt the universal habit of the place, and call for a mint julep, a whiskey skin, a gin cock-tail, a brandy smash, or a glass of pure Old Rye, for the conviviality of Washington sets in at an early hour and, so far as I had an opportunity of observing, never terminates at any hour."[30]

Whitman frequented the Willard on occasion, stopping there for a respite during his hospital rounds, but he did not always appreciate the many officers who crowded the lobby. He wrote a possibly imaginary scene in *Memoranda* about the July 1861 Battle of Bull Run, in which he laid the blame for the Union's loss on the officer corps that was more interested in being seen at the Willard than in leading their men. He described the hotel as "full of shoulder-straps—thick, crush'd, creeping with shoulder-straps. (I see them, and must have a word with them. There you are, shoulder-straps!—but where are your companies? where are your men? Incompetents!…)"[31]

Most of Washington was soggy wet—it was a wet, wet capital, with alcohol being at the center of many social occasions. Saloons and taverns were where men whiled away their evenings. Walt was no different, though he drank much less than men of his day. In 1842, he wrote a temperance novel called *Franklin Evans*, but his fervor for dryness soon receded. He acquired a taste for lager at Pfaff's in Manhattan and was known to sip beer in Washington as well. Walt's partner Peter Doyle recalled, "He was a very moderate drinker. You might have thought something different, to see the ruddiness of his complexion—but his complexion had no whiskey in it." Whitman didn't smoke. He detested tobacco, though he frequently bought tobacco for soldiers.[32]

Across Pennsylvania Avenue was a neighborhood that decent folk didn't frequent. It was built on lowland that paralleled the stinking Washington City Canal and went by the inauspicious but appropriate name of Murder Bay (it is today the Federal Triangle). Many former slaves and impoverished immigrants resided in its shanties. The neighborhood was a lawless part of the city that earned its nickname. It was also known as Hooker's Division for its concentration of bordellos.

Washington was either choking in dust or drowning in mud, as few of the streets had been paved. Streets were littered with horse manure from the many carriages and horsecars (at the time, they were called "horsecars" rather than streetcars, as a horse pulled them), making them ill suited for pedestrians. The railroad that passed through the Mall, as well as the coal-powered steamships that brought the wounded up the Potomac River, rained coal dust on the city. Coal was the primary way people heated their houses.

The bustling Georgetown waterfront during the Civil War. *Library of Congress.*

To get in and out of wartime Washington, whether by boat or by train, travel passes were required. The main railroad link to the north began at the B&O Railroad station just north of the Capitol in the Irish ghetto known as Swampoodle. The U.S. Sanitary Commission opened a Soldiers' Rest near the train station for Union soldiers. It wasn't a hospital but rather a place for soldiers to rest, get a meal and take a bed during a furlough. It also became a temporary home for invalid soldiers. There was a similar Soldiers' Rest near the Alexandria train station. Whitman never made mention of visiting either station; then again, he had a strong dislike of the U.S. Sanitary Commission.

Washington was not a large city, and it was clustered in just a few neighborhoods. Capitol Hill was the crown of the city, but surrounding it were houses for workers at the Navy Yard, the hill's largest employer. Along the Potomac was the Waterfront with its many piers. The Sixth Street Wharf was the busiest in the city and was where the ships loaded with wounded soldiers docked. Beyond the Smithsonian Castle, there wasn't much to see on the National Mall except military hospitals, railroad tracks and shanties. Even Georgetown, the oldest settlement in the district, was a working-class neighborhood where the C&O Canal ended, and factories lined the canal to take advantage of its water supply.

Many visitors were critical of Washington's vast distances and empty spaces, but Whitman fell in love with the city. An 1863 article he penned for the *New York Times* was practically a love letter to Washington. He found it an exciting city with the bustle of war and yet with serene views and grand spaces for walking. "I continually enjoy these streets, planned on such a generous scale, stretching far, without stop or turn, giving the eye vistas. I feel freer, larger in them." He had spent much of his life in crowded Brooklyn and Manhattan, but now he had room to spread out. "I often find it silently, curiously making up to me the absence of the ocean tumult of humanity I always enjoyed in New-York. Here, too, is largeness, in another more impalpable form; and I never walk Washington, day or night, without feeling its satisfaction." He concluded: "But this city, even in the crude state it is to-day, with its buildings of to-day, with its ample river and its streets,

A detail-rich image from 1863 shows the corner of Seventh and D Streets Northwest. Photographer Alexander Gardner's gallery is upstairs while on the ground floor is Shepherd & Riley's Bookstore, where Walt Whitman shopped for writing accoutrements. Clara Barton's relief office is just out of the picture to the left. Note the horsecar tracks in the foreground along Seventh Street. *Library of Congress.*

with the effects above noted, to say nothing of what it all represents, is of course greater, materially and morally to-day than ever Rome or Athens."[33]

Washington was a city you could walk across in an hour or two. Starting in 1862, however, horse-drawn streetcar lines crisscrossed the city and could transport people faster than walking—and without pedestrians having to stroll in the filthy streets. The streets with horsecars were at least paved with cobblestones, though there was just as much—if not more—horse manure.

Then there were the constant caravans of army wagons: convoys hauling munitions and supplies, teams of oxen pulling heavy artillery and, always, the ever-present ambulances transporting the wounded to the hospitals. Walt illustrated it for the *New York Times*: "Washington may be described as the city of army wagons also. These are on the go at all times, in all streets, and everywhere around here for many a mile. You see long trains of thirty, fifty, a hundred, and even two hundred. It seems as if they never would come to an end."[34] The army wagons were a constant reminder that the country was at war and that Washington could at any moment be on the front line if the tide turned against the Union.

A Union ambulance train at Harewood Hospital. *Library of Congress.*

WHITMAN SETTLES IN

The day after returning to Washington from Fredericksburg, Whitman wrote to Ralph Waldo Emerson, asking (or more like demanding) that he write three letters of recommendation for federal employment "on literary grounds, not political." Walt aimed high: these were to be addressed to Secretary of State William Seward, Secretary of the Treasury Salmon Chase and Senator Charles Sumner, asking them to provide a job for Whitman.[35] Emerson obliged. Whitman ended up not presenting the letters—they weren't a strong endorsement—except to Sumner. Sumner met with Whitman but couldn't or wouldn't help, and he instead referred him to Whitman's own senator, Preston King.

Walt paid a visit to Senator King in the Senate to ask for a job. Whitman was apparently dressed in his bohemian garb, as King promptly declared, "Why, how can I do this thing, or any thing for you—how do I know but you are a secessionist—you look for all the world, like an old Southern planter—a regular Carolina or Virginia planter." King did little for him, though after meeting Walt a second time, he grudgingly provided a general endorsement that proved useless.[36]

Whitman had some connections. When he decided to stay in Washington for relief work, he took a part-time job as a copyist in early 1863. The man who hired him was his publisher, Charles Eldridge, who was the assistant to the army paymaster, Major Lyman Hapgood. Whitman took up his pen for the federal government at his new desk in the Corcoran Office Building (now the site of the W Hotel Washington). The job allowed him just enough money to pay his rent while also providing plenty of spare time for him to minister to soldiers. The paymaster's office had a gorgeous view of the city from its location on the fifth floor of the Corcoran Building. On February 15, Whitman watched the sun go down on a winter's day, as he penned in a notebook:

> *A long string of army wagons are defiling along 15th street, and around into Pennsylvania avenue—white canvas coverings arch them over, and each one has its six-mule team—the teamsters are some of them walking along by the sides of their animals—squads of the provost-guard are tramping frequently along—and once or twice a party of cavalry in their yellow-trimmed jacks gallop along—I see sick and wounded soldiers, (but that's nothing new—I have seen so many thousands of them)—the light falls, falls, touches the cold white of the great public edifices—touches with a kind of death-glaze here and there the windows of Washington.[37]*

A team of oxen hauls a Rodman gun along Pennsylvania Avenue past the Corcoran Building on Fifteenth Street Northwest, home of the Army Paymaster's Office. *Historical Society of Washington, D.C.*

In addition to working for the army paymaster, Whitman also worked as a freelance journalist for the *New York Times*, thanks to his friend John Swinton, who was the editor there. The articles earned him some income, in addition to his part-time job and donations that covered his basic costs and enabled him to buy supplies for his hospital visits. The articles that Walt wrote formed the basis for his book *Memoranda During the War* (1876).

Walt's brother George was the primary source of income for their mother during the Civil War. Walt's income was sporadic until he gained federal employment in 1865. He always sent his mother something, but she relied on George's army pay to support her and the household in Brooklyn.

THE PATENT OFFICE

Walt Whitman is associated with the Patent Office more than any other building in Washington. Not only did he work in the building in 1865, but

Top: An 1846 daguerreotype of the Patent Office. *Library of Congress.*

Bottom: This lithograph shows an idealized Patent Office circa 1855. *Library of Congress.*

Opposite, top: This 1869 engraving shows patent examiners at work in the Patent Office. *Library of Congress.*

Opposite, bottom: The First Rhode Island Regiment was lodged in the Patent Office during the opening months of the Civil War in 1861. *Library of Congress.*

he also made many visits to wounded soldiers as the building served as a temporary hospital. In fairness, the building could be equally associated with Clara Barton, who began working there in 1854.

Construction on the building began in 1836, and wings were added as its collection grew and the demand for patents increased. The building eventually enclosed an open-air courtyard. "You may approach it from four opposite directions, and on each side you lift your eyes to four sublime porticoes towering before you," wrote Mary Clemmer Ames in 1873.[38] All four sides resembled the Parthenon in Athens, and the Patent Office is considered the most prominent Greek Revival building in Washington.

Many patents were for mechanical inventions, and applicants had to submit models of their ideas to the patent examiners. These models then went on display in cases and shelves, and soon the Patent Office had become an informal museum to many early Washington tourists. Galleries on the upper two floors displayed patent models while the lower floors were reserved for offices. *Boyd's Washington Directory* described the Patent Office: "Here the visitor may see the models of the countless machines which have grown out of the inventive Yankee brain."[39]

The Patent Office also had some of the largest public space in Washington, which is why it was used for many public events, including Lincoln's second inaugural ball, and why it served as a temporary barracks and hospital during the Civil War.

With the start of the Civil War, Union soldiers poured in to protect Washington. The First Rhode Island Regiment was housed in the Patent Office in 1861. It stayed two months before the Battle of Bull Run. The soldiers lodged on the third floor among the patent model cases, breaking four hundred of the glass cases. Many of the patent models disappeared.

In 1862, up to two thousand temporary hospital beds were set up in the Patent Office, and President Lincoln sometimes paid the wounded a visit. Clara Barton tended to the wounded housed there. By 1863, the temporary hospital had closed, as the military had built general hospitals around the city that could better handle the wounded.

Whitman described the Patent Office as "that noblest of Washington buildings."[40] When he began his soldiers' missionary work in early 1863, the second story of the building was being used as a temporary hospital, and the wounded were intermingled with the glass cases that held the patent models. He described the scene for the *New York Times*:

This Civil War–era graffiti carved into a windowsill of the Patent Office was discovered during the Smithsonian American Art Museum's 2000–06 renovation. It reads, "C.H.F—1864 Aug 8th." *Garrett Peck.*

The glass cases, the beds, the sick, the gallery above and the marble pavement under foot—the suffering, and the fortitude to bear it in various degrees—occasionally, from some, the groan that could not be repressed—sometimes a poor fellow dying, with emaciated face and glassy eye, the nurse by his side, the doctor also there, but no friend, no relative—such were the sights but lately in the Patent Office. The wounded have since been removed from there, and it is now vacant again.[41]

The Patent Office eventually became the Smithsonian American Art Museum and National Portrait Gallery. It closed for a six-year renovation that largely restored the building to its historic configuration. It reopened in 2006. The Sir Norman Foster–designed roof was added the next year. One of the discoveries during the renovation was of Civil War–era graffiti, carved into a windowsill on the floor where the Lincoln inaugural ball was held. The graffiti includes the initials C.H.F., as well as the date: "1864 Aug 8th." A glass plate now protects the graffiti.

No one knows who carved the graffiti. Was it a Civil War soldier, a doctor, nurse or patient? The Patent Office continued to function as a museum during the war, including during the time when the graffiti was carved. It could have simply been a tourist.

WHERE DID WHITMAN LIVE IN WASHINGTON?

Walt Whitman never had many possessions, nor was he ever rich. He lived quite modestly in seven different boardinghouses during his decade in Washington, D.C. He would generally visit his family in Brooklyn every summer, saving him a month's rent, and when he returned to Washington, he would move into a new boardinghouse. The addresses shown were the old street numbering convention. Unfortunately, none of the buildings survives: all were located downtown and were torn down for redevelopment. According to historian Kim Roberts, Whitman lived at the following locations:

* 394 L Street North (now 1100 Vermont Avenue Northwest). Whitman sublet a second-floor bedroom from his close friends William and Nelly O'Connor for seven dollars per month starting in January 1863. From this location, Whitman frequently saw President Lincoln riding to or from the Soldiers' Home. Whitman disliked the landlord, Carey Gwynne. When Gwynne sold the house, the O'Connors and Whitman had to move in October.

* 456 Sixth Street West (now the Securities and Exchange Commission at 415 Sixth Street Northwest). Whitman rented the attic from Eliza Baker, a widow, in October 1863 for ten dollars per month. He was

the only boarder in the house, and he was pleased to have privacy. The O'Connors had moved just down the street, and Whitman continued to dine with them nightly. John Trowbridge visited him there.

- 502 Pennsylvania Avenue (now on the grounds of the U.S. Capitol). Whitman rented a miserable apartment in May 1864 near the fetid Washington Canal, which was an open sewer. He complained about what it did to his health, yet it was close to the Armory Square Hospital, where he often volunteered. Whitman rented the room for just one month: he took an extended break from the war in June 1864, moving back to Brooklyn until January 1865.

- 468 M Street North (now the Claridge Tower Apartments at 1221 M Street Northwest). Whitman returned to Washington in January 1865 to start his job as a federal clerk. He rented a large room from Edward and Juliet Grayson for $32.50 per month and found the landlords to be charming and good cooks. During this time, he met Peter Doyle.

- 364 Thirteenth Street West (now 1220 L Street Northwest). Whitman moved to this location in February 1866.

- 472 M Street North (now the Claridge Tower Apartments at 1221 M Street Northwest). Just a few doors up from his former lodgings, this boardinghouse became Whitman's residence sometime in 1867. His landlady was Newton Benedict, who worked for the Treasury Department. Many young people also boarded at the house. It was the longest Washington residence that Whitman had (around three years). He remained there until he returned to New York in July 1870 to oversee the publication of three titles: *Democratic Vistas, Leaves of Grass* (fifth edition) and *Passage to India*.

- 535 Fifteenth Street Northwest (now the W Washington Hotel). No one is certain when Whitman moved into this house, which was near the Treasury Building, where he worked. His room was a cold attic, so Whitman spent many days in the office to keep warm. It was there that he suffered his first stroke in January 1873, and he permanently left Washington several months later.[42]

In 1930, *Washington Post* columnist George Rothwell Brown wrote about one of Whitman's apartments as a historic site but did not identify which one it was:

> *The little house where Whitman lived the greater part of the time he was in Washington during the Civil War was no sacred shrine to the literary celebrities of the town in the Seventies, Eighties or Nineties, nor has it become a shrine even to this day, although it is still standing, much altered*

in appearance, but none the less the humble abode that once sheltered the greatest American poet since Poe. No tourists visit it, and no bronze tablet, nor even a wooden sign, marks the spot.[43]

CONTRABANDS

One thing was absent from the city of Washington when Whitman arrived in December 1862: slaves. The Compensated Emancipation Act of April 16, 1862, had purchased the freedom of the remaining three thousand slaves still in the nation's capital. This day became an annual district holiday known as Emancipation Day. On January 1, 1863, President Lincoln signed the Emancipation Proclamation, targeting the slaves in states that were in rebellion. It was the beginning of the end for slavery. Whitman had returned from Fredericksburg just four days before.

Perched atop a hill across the Potomac River in Virginia was a striking Greek Revival mansion known as Arlington House. It was the center of a

This photograph of Arlington House is dated June 28, 1864, thirteen days after the official founding of Arlington National Cemetery. *Library of Congress.*

Freedman's Village was founded on the grounds south of Arlington House. Alfred Waugh sketched this drawing, published in *Harper's Weekly* on May 7, 1864. *Library of Congress.*

1,100-acre plantation. Its owner, Robert E. Lee, resigned his commission in the U.S. Army when his home state of Virginia seceded, and he moved to Richmond to take command of Virginia's military forces. The abandoned plantation and its prominent high ground were tempting targets for the federal government.

On May 24, 1861—the day after Virginia seceded—Union forces in Washington crossed the Potomac River into Virginia and occupied the high ground to protect the city from Confederate attack and to guard the three bridges into the city. The abandoned Arlington House became a Union army headquarters, and the garrison made an encampment of the plantation. Mary Anna Custis Lee's (Robert E. Lee's wife) famous rose garden was destroyed. The house was open to the public.

Whitman never mentioned Arlington House, but he probably did visit. He often ventured to the Virginia side of the Potomac River and even wrote in the *New York Times*, "I have stood over on the Virginia hills" admiring the view of the city. He was also well acquainted with the army camps on the Lee property. Walt also made at least one visit to George Washington's home at Mount Vernon.[44]

The Union forts protecting the capital were often crowded with contraband camps, as the former slaves had nowhere else to go. To help alleviate their plight, a Freedman's Village was established on the Lee-Custis plantation in June 1863. It was a proper town with schools and civic responsibilities, where people could learn new skills now that they were off the plantation. Sojourner Truth worked for a time at Freedman's Village. The site, now part of Arlington National Cemetery, was dismantled in 1900.

Chapter 3

THE WOUND-DRESSER

In January 1863, Walt Whitman wrote a rather poetic letter to Ralph Waldo Emerson—more formal than the letters he usually addressed to his mother or his brothers. After observing the tens of thousands of young men crowding the hospitals of Washington, D.C., he wrote, "America, already brought to Hospital in her fair youth."[45]

Despite the many newspaper accounts of battles and future biographies that would be written, Whitman realized one fundamental truth about war: it was a deeply violent encounter grasped truly by only those who witnessed it firsthand, and even then, no words could convey the experience. He wrote in *Memoranda*: "Future years will never know the seething hell and the black infernal background of countless minor scenes and interiors, (not the few great battles) of the Secession War; and it is best they should not." He added: "Its interior history will not only never be written, its practicality, minutia of deeds and passions, will never be even suggested."[46] Whitman rewrote this last sentence more concisely in his autobiography, *Specimen Days*: "The real war will never get in the books."[47]

Walt never experienced a battle, having seen only the army camps, but he witnessed firsthand the horrible human toll from the Civil War. Washington had become a massive hospital ward. It was there that he found his calling to serve as a soldiers' missionary. He soon realized there were more sick soldiers in the hospitals than there were wounded. Walt would later say, "That whole damned war business is about nine hundred and ninety nine parts diarrhea to one part glory."[48]

CIVIL WAR MEDICINE

During the Civil War, the Union adopted a three-tier medical system for the wounded. A wounded soldier was carried to a field dressing station on the battlefield. A regimental surgeon administered morphine or whiskey and bandaged his wounds, and then the soldier was carried to a field hospital behind the army's lines.

The field hospital was often in a barn or house, and there the wounded were triaged into lightly wounded, need surgery or mortally wounded. The field hospital was where most amputations took place. The Civil War armies used lead bullets that shattered bones, leaving surgeons with only one choice if they wished to save a soldier's life: amputation. Surgeons anesthetized soldiers with chloroform or ether and then removed the wounded appendage. Amputation was brutal but effective, and if done quickly, it could prevent gangrene or other infection.

After surgery, soldiers faced a long recovery. They were transported by rail or ship to a general hospital, large facilities that could support thousands of soldiers and that were concentrated in Baltimore, Philadelphia and Washington. The wounded who were expected to recover and rejoin their army units remained in Washington while those who would be discharged were gradually moved to more northern hospitals.

A field hospital at the Battle of Chancellorsville. *Library of Congress.*

WASHINGTON'S HOSPITALS

At the peak of the Civil War, Washington hospitals treated eighteen thousand wounded, and more than forty hospitals operated in the city. They ranged from pavilion-style general hospitals to temporary facilities in government buildings to quite a number of churches. Some hospitals, such as Campbell and Carver, had originally served as barracks. The large number of hospitals reflected how unprepared the army was for the casualties, and how improvised medical treatment was in the early part of the war.[49]

As the war progressed, however, the Union made necessary reforms to the hospital system, thanks largely to the U.S. Sanitary Commission, the country's official relief organization. The commission organized pavilion hospitals designed by landscape architect Frederick Law Olmsted. These hospitals, organized into wings with good lighting and sanitary conditions, were first introduced during the Crimean War, a decade earlier. Pavilion hospitals took on the greatest numbers of wounded, allowing the temporary hospitals, such as churches and the Patent Office, to resume their regular functions. The six pavilion hospitals in Washington included Armory Square, Harewood, Judiciary Square, Lincoln, Mount Pleasant and Stanton Hospitals.

Whitman described the extensive hospital network that covered Washington. From a vantage point above the city, he could see hospitals

Mount Pleasant U.S. General Hospital was one of many Civil War–era hospitals in Washington, D.C. *Library of Congress.*

in every direction, and together they could hold fifty to seventy thousand patients. He described the setting in *Memoranda*:

That little town, as you might suppose it, off there on the brow of a hill, is indeed a town, but of wounds, sickness, and death. It is Finley Hospital, northeast of the city, on Kendall Green, as it used to be call'd. That other is Campbell Hospital. Both are large establishments. I have known these two alone to have from two thousand to twenty-five hundred inmates. Then there is Carver Hospital, larger still, a wall'd and military city regularly laid out, and guarded by squads of sentries. Again, off east, Lincoln Hospital, a still larger one; and half a mile further Emory hospital. Still seeping the eye around down the river toward Alexandria, we see, to the right, the locality where the Convalescent Camp stands, with its five, eight, or sometimes ten thousand inmates. Even all these are but a portion. The Harewood, Mount Pleasant, Armory Square, Judiciary Hospitals, are some of the rest, and all large collections.[50]

Walt didn't limit his hospital visits to just Washington. He sometimes ventured across the river to visit the thousands of wounded in Virginia. Alexandria County (now Arlington) was home to the Convalescent Camp south of Long Bridge (later upgraded to Augur General Hospital) in what is now the Nauck neighborhood. The city of Alexandria had several hospitals as well, including the Mansion House Hospital (Carlyle House) and Sickle Hospital near Fairfax Seminary (now Virginia Theological Seminary). Both of these buildings still stand.

In Washington today, only a handful of buildings survive that served as Civil War hospitals, including the Patent Office (National Portrait Gallery); the Seminary Hospital in Georgetown; St. Elizabeths in Anacostia; a fair number of churches; and the Old Naval Hospital (921 Pennsylvania Avenue Southeast) on Capitol Hill, founded in 1866 to replace the Marine Hospital at the Navy Yard. The record doesn't indicate if Whitman ever visited this latter hospital, built to support marines and sailors, though it was close to the horsecar line. It opened as Walt was wrapping up his hospital visits.

After a major battle, the wounded streamed into the city by ship, docking at the Sixth and Seventh Street Wharves; by ambulance, loaded into horse-drawn wagons; or by railroad, offloaded at the Maryland Avenue depot (now L'Enfant Plaza). They came from the front in Virginia, fifty or more miles away. They suffered long before they found a bed in Washington.

The Old Naval Hospital opened in 1866 as Whitman was wrapping up his hospital visits. It now serves as the Hill Center, a Capitol Hill community center. *Garrett Peck.*

Union wounded arrived by ship at the Sixth Street Wharf in Southwest, where they were offloaded and sent to hospitals. *Library of Congress.*

An 1863 view of Washington from the Capitol. The white pavilions of Armory Square Hospital are clearly visible on the Mall, just below the Smithsonian Castle. On the right, the fetid Washington Canal separates Southwest (the "Island") from the rest of the city. *Library of Congress*.

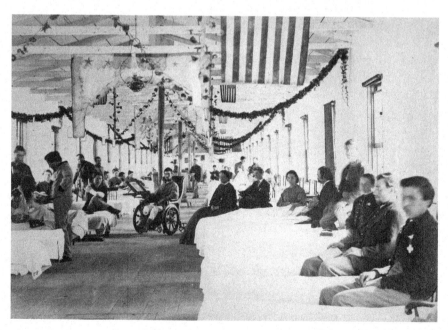

A hospital ward crowded with soldiers and visitors. Note the pine branches strung from the ceiling to freshen the air. *Library of Congress*.

Armory Square Hospital was a pavilion-style Civil War hospital on the National Mall. Walt Whitman visited this hospital more than any other. *Library of Congress.*

Armory Square Hospital had eleven wards, lettered A through K. Whitman met Oscar Cunningham in Ward K. *Library of Congress.*

Ambulances fanned out across the city, often in wagon trains counted by the dozen, dropping the wounded off at the many hospitals. The streets were crowded with wagons making the endless rounds between the Waterfront and the hospitals, the ambulances driven by teamsters who lived in their wagons and led a "wild, hard life," Walt noted. Many were invalids themselves. "You mark the forms huddled on the bottom of these wagons; you mark yellow and emaciated faces. Some are supporting others. I constantly see instances of tenderness in this way from the wounded to those worse wounded."[51]

From the wharves of Waterfront, the closest hospital was Armory Square. It was built adjacent to the Washington Armory on the National Mall. It had eleven wards, lettered A through K. Whitman wrote to his mother that Armory Square was the place he visited most: "I devote myself much to Armory Square Hospital because it contains by far the worst cases, most repulsive wounds, has the most suffering & most need of consolation—I go every day without fail, & often at night—sometimes stay very late—no one interferes with me, guards, doctors, nurses, nor any one—I am let to take my own course."[52] The hospital is now the site of the National Air and Space Museum.

WHITMAN AT THE HOSPITALS

Whitman began his hospital visits in January 1863, continuing until the last hospital shut down in 1866. He claimed in *Memoranda*: "During those three years in hospital, camp or field, I made over six hundred visits and tours, and went, as I estimate, counting all, among from eighty thousand to a hundred thousand of the wounded and sick, as sustainer of spirit and body."[53]

Before Whitman visited a hospital, he bathed, ate dinner and put on his nicest clothes—a red wine–colored suit—so as to present the best appearance for the soldiers. He abandoned his baggy bohemian attire and began dressing up, even putting on a necktie. Walt was fastidiously clean. He steeled himself for the ordeal of supporting the sick and wounded. He needed to present his most cheerful best. "In my visits to the Hospitals I found it was in the simple matter of Personal Presence, and emanating ordinary cheer and magnetism, that I succeeded and help'd more than by medical nursing, or delicacies, or gifts of money, or anything else," he wrote.[54]

Whitman was like everyone's favorite uncle, a surrogate brother or father. A bear of a man with his bushy gray beard and receding hairline that made him appear older than he was, Walt was charming and easy-going, and quite compassionate with the many wounded he encountered. Whitman thought his appearance put the men at ease, as he wrote to his mother: "The reason I am able to do some good in the hospitals, among the poor languishing & wounded boys, is that I am so large and well—indeed like a great wild buffalo, with much hair."[55]

Washington summers are oppressively hot and humid, and yet most men wore wool suits, often of black. Whitman was heavyset and probably sweated a lot; he always had difficulty in the heat. He took to carrying a fan and an umbrella to shield himself from the sun. His complexion was ruddy, and he often looked sunburned.

Walt could just as freely mix with polite society, literary circles and politicians as he could make friends with the working class—with whom he is keenly associated—and the largely teenage and twenty-something soldiers who were the backbone of the Union army. That he would have been attracted to some of these young men goes without saying, and Whitman (and some of the soldiers) may have found some sexual release. But more likely he sublimated his sexual desires through service.

Whitman didn't so much nurse the soldiers as minister to them, providing a welcoming ear—he was a good listener—a shoulder to lean on and his friendship (he is sometimes referred to as a nurse, but more accurately, he was a hospital volunteer. There were paid nurses on duty, and Whitman was never a nurse). Whitman was a gentle man and kind to everyone. His compassion drove him to serve the tens of thousands of wounded in the hospital wards. He always marveled at the bravery of these teenagers, even when their deaths were inevitable.

One of the first soldiers that Walt helped was John Holmes, a private from Plymouth, Massachusetts. Whitman had ventured to Campbell Hospital on January 2, 1863, to check on two Brooklyn soldiers when he encountered Holmes in the same ward. The boy was pallid and glassy eyed, suffering from bronchitis, diarrhea and vomiting. Walt described the visit to his sister-in-law Mattie: "I talked to him some time—he seemed to have entirely given up, and lost heart—he had not a cent of money—not a friend or acquaintance—I wrote a letter from him to his sister…I gave him a little change I had—he said he would like to buy a drink of milk, when the woman came through with milk. Trifling as this was, he was overcome and began to cry."[56]

Whitman would write about this encounter in the first article he wrote for the *New York Times*, called "The Great Army of the Sick." He described how the soldier, identified by the initials J.A.H., was transported by train on an open platform in late December 1862 and then taken by steamer to Washington, where he was so weak he couldn't wrap himself in a blanket and no one would help. He was thrown like a rag into a hospital bed and ignored. "His heart was broken. He felt the struggle to keep up any longer to be useless. God, the world, humanity—all had abandoned him. It would feel so good to shut his eyes forever on the cruel things around him and toward him," Whitman wrote. "As luck would have it, at this time, I found him." Walt spoke with the young man, who didn't respond at first, but after Walt's attentions, he began talking. Over the course of the next month, Holmes's health improved. "He has told me since that this little visit, at that hour, just saved him—a day more, and it would have been perhaps too late."[57]

Walt followed this up with another article, "The Great Washington Hospitals: Life Among Fifty Thousand Soldiers," for the *Brooklyn Daily Eagle* on March 19. He described his work as a "hospital missionary," singling out the many soldiers from Brooklyn whom he had visited.[58]

Walt wrote to his brother Jeff about his hospital visits: "I never before had my feelings so thoroughly and (so far) permanently absorbed, to the very roots, as by these huge swarms of dear, wounded, sick, dying boys—I get very much attached to some of them, and many of them have come to depend on seeing me, and having me sit by them a few minutes, as if for their lives."[59] Two weeks later, he wrote to Jeff about an odd feeling in his head, "a bad humming feeling and deafness, stupor-like at times," which he attributed to a bad cold. It was perhaps an early symptom of the hypertension that would lead to Whitman's stroke a decade later.[60]

A Union officer, John Brown associate and radical abolitionist named Richard Hinton became a Whitman friend and defender. Hinton had been wounded at Antietam and was hospitalized for months in Washington afterward. He met Whitman when Walt was just beginning his hospital visits. Hinton recalled Walt's way with the soldiers in an 1871 article in the *Cincinnati Commercial*. On Sundays, the hospital wards were crowded with Christian proselytizers, much to the annoyance of the soldiers. But Walt made no effort to convert anyone—he was an "old heathen," as Hinton called him. "A wounded soldier don't like to be reminded of his God more than twenty times a day," he wrote. "Walt Whitman didn't have any tracts or Bibles, he didn't ask if you love the Lord, and didn't seem to care whether you did or not. But he did bring you pipes and tobacco and interesting books, and all such worldly items."[61]

Only when a dying soldier asked for a reading from the Bible did Walt turn to this book. Such was the case with Oscar Wilder, a wounded man who was also suffering from severe diarrhea, who asked Walt to read aloud a passage about Jesus's death and resurrection. Whitman described the scene in the *New York Times*: "It pleased him very much, yet the tears were in his eyes. He asked me if I enjoyed religion. I said: 'Perhaps not, my dear, in the way you mean, and yet, may-be, it is the same thing.' He said: 'It is my chief reliance.' He talked of death, and said he did not fear it. I said: 'Why, OSCAR, don't you think you will get well?' He said: "I may, but it is not probable.' He spoke calmly of his condition."[62]

Walt made many appeals for funds throughout New England and New York to support his hospital ministry. His brother Jeff became his chief fundraiser, soliciting contributions at the Brooklyn Water Works. The chief engineer, Moses Lane, was particularly generous, once remarking, "We ought [to] raise money enough to keep a 100 Walt Whitmans."[63] Walt often wrote to his financial supporters with the details of his hospital visits, and they responded in kind with donations. He wrote to thank a financial supporter, William Davis, who had sent him fifty dollars:

> *I always carry a haversack with some articles most wanted—physical comforts are a sort of basis. I distribute nice large biscuit, sweet-crackers, sometimes cut up a lot of peaches with sugar, give preserves of all kinds, jellies, &c. tea, oysters, butter, condensed milk, plugs of tobacco. (I am the only one that doles out this last, & the men have grown to look to me.)—wine, brandy, sugar, pickles, letter-stamps, envelopes & note-paper, the morning paper, common handkerchiefs & napkins, undershirts, socks, dressing gowns, & fifty other things—I have lots of special little requests.*[64]

Walt often distributed stamped envelopes and paper, or if a soldier couldn't write, he would transcribe a letter for him. In some cases, he gave small sums of money, as most soldiers arrived at the hospitals without a cent on them. He often carried jelly, a large pot for an entire ward. "Many want tobacco; I do not encourage any of the boys in its use, but where I find they crave it I supply them," he wrote in a newspaper article.[65] In order to jot down ideas and keep track of each soldier's needs, Walt created dozens of small notebooks, "each composed of a sheet or two of paper, folded small to

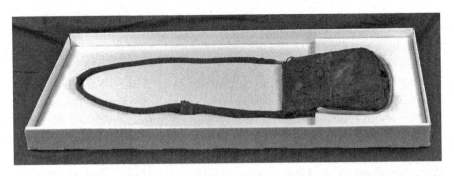

The leather haversack that Walt Whitman used to carry provisions for tens of thousands of hospitalized soldiers is part of the Library of Congress's extensive Whitman collection. It is in fragile condition. *Library of Congress.*

carry in the pocket, and fasten'd with a pin," as he described them. Most of these surviving notebooks are in the Library of Congress.[66]

Whitman's friend and first biographer, John Burroughs, occasionally accompanied Walt on his hospital visits. He noted that Walt never brought up that he was a poet, and that contributed to a certain air of mystery. Burroughs humorously wrote that Whitman was often confused for someone else: "Now he was a benevolent Catholic priest—then some unknown army general, or retired sea captain; and at one time he was the owner of the whole Cunard line of steamers. To be taken for a Californian had been common."[67]

Whitman's great, shaggy white beard reminded some of Santa Claus, especially in the winter. Nelly O'Connor recalled one evening when Walt was returning from Carver Hospital. "He was accosted by a policeman and ordered to remove that 'false face,' his name for a mask. Walt quietly assured him that the only face he wore was his very own, but added, 'Do we not all wear 'false faces'?"[68]

When spring arrived in 1863, the Union armies prepared to move against the Confederacy. A torrent of casualties arrived in Washington in May after the Union defeat at Chancellorsville. Walt noted that people were growing callous toward the wounded, and hospital attendants were even stealing money from their charges.[69]

After his victory at Chancellorsville, Confederate general Robert E. Lee invaded the North, but he was decisively defeated at Gettysburg (July 1–3, 1863). The day after the battle ended, Whitman made his rounds with a special treat to help the soldiers celebrate the victory: "I walk'd on to Armory Hospital—took along with me several bottles of blackberry and cherry syrup, good and strong, but innocent [meaning: no alcohol]. Went through several of the Wards, announc'd to the soldiers the news from Meade, and gave them all a good drink of the syrups with ice water, quite refreshing."[70]

Few of the Gettysburg casualties made it to Washington hospitals; instead, they were sent to Philadelphia. Walt wrote to his mother just days after the battle. While others celebrated, Walt privately mourned for the thousands of dead and the many wounded: "Mother, one's heart grows sick of war, after all, when you see what it really is—every once in a while I feel so horrified & disgusted."[71]

After the Emancipation Proclamation, the Union began arming former slaves and organizing men into army regiments. This was a significant source of manpower against the Confederacy, as some 200,000 African Americans fought for the Union. On June 30, 1863, the First District Colored Volunteers became the First Regiment United States Colored Troops (USCT). These black soldiers were now Federal troops. They were stationed on Mason's Island (now Roosevelt Island) in the Potomac River, across from Georgetown. That same day, Whitman penned a long letter to his mother about the Confederate offensive that would lead to Gettysburg and what it was like seeing Abraham Lincoln and concluded by mentioning the black soldiers: "There are getting to be *many black troops*—there is one very good reg't here black as tar—they go armed, have the regular uniform—they submit to no nonsense—others are constantly forming—it is getting to be a common sight—they press them."[72]

Around the time of Gettysburg, Whitman went with the army paymaster's staff to Mason's Island to pay the First Regiment USCT. Hapgood invited not only his assistant Charles Eldridge and Whitman but also William and Nelly O'Connor and their daughter Jeannie. Nelly considered the occasion historic.[73] Whitman wrote to his mother: "They make a good show, are often seen in the streets of Washington in squads—since they have begun to carry arms, the secesh here & in Georgetown (about 3/5ths) [of Washington's population] are not insulting to them as formerly."[74]

Walt claimed he was equally attentive to Southern soldiers as he was to Northern soldiers in his hospital visits. "I can say that in my ministerings I comprehended all, whoever came in my way, Northern or Southern, and slighted none," he summarized at the end of *Memoranda*. He helped many Rebel soldiers, as well as Union patients and teamsters. "Among the black soldiers, wounded or sick, and in the contraband camps, I also took my way whenever in their neighborhood, and did what I could for them."[75] Here

Whitman was being less than genuine: his letters and prose indicates a sharp preference for white Union soldiers. His writings rarely mentioned helping black soldiers. Walt's attitudes about race were not uncommon for white Northerners of his time, who, even though they opposed slavery, still saw the United States as a white country.[76]

Chapter 4
NURSES, STEWARDS & SURGEONS

Washington's military hospitals were essentially open to everyone—family, friends, proselytizers—who came to visit the wounded. Whitman was one of the few civilians who established close relationships with the surgeons, stewards and nurses of the hospital wards. Most learned to appreciate his presence as a positive force in the soldiers' morale, and he, in turn, realized how committed they were to their patients.

Whitman greatly admired the lengths to which the surgeons would go to save a man's life. "I have noticed through most of the hospitals that as long as there is any chance for a man, no matter how bad he may be, the surgeon and nurses work hard, sometimes with curious tenacity, for his life, doing everything, and keeping somebody by him to execute the doctor's orders, and minister to him every minute night and day," he wrote.[77]

Many doctors come up in Walt's correspondence, but none so frequently as Dr. Willard Bliss, the chief surgeon at Armory Square Hospital, whom Whitman considered a friend. Walt wrote to a dead soldier's parents that Dr. Bliss was "one of the best surgeons in the army."[78] Bliss likewise had great admiration for Walt, about whom he later said, "No one person who assisted in the hospitals during the war accomplished so much good to the soldiers and for the Government as Mr. Whitman."[79] Whitman seemed to have a strong stomach: he watched many surgeries, always with fascination. He even helped with one procedure, though he was accidentally nicked by the surgeon's knife in the hand, which grew infected.

The mess hall at Harewood Hospital. *Library of Congress.*

The great majority of Civil War nurses were men, often wounded soldiers who were delegated to the medical corps. There were also many women who served. The role of women was subtly changing as a result of the war, as women took on more responsibility on the homefront in the absence of brothers, fathers and husbands. There were no nursing schools yet or formal training programs for nurses. Most nurses received their training at the hospital itself.

Whitman was ahead of his time in advocating for women's dignity, but usually within the context of motherhood, which he put on a pedestal. He advocated for more female nurses, especially for older, more matronly nurses, believing that a mother's instinct would serve best in a hospital full of wounded teenagers. "The presence of a good middle-aged or elderly woman, the magnetic touch of hands, the expressive features of the mother, the silent soothing of her presence, her words, her knowledge and privileges arrived at only through having had children, are precious and final qualifications," he wrote.[80]

Whitman's letters often mentioned the female nurses he met during his hospital visits. Sometimes they even leaned on Walt in distress or in grief.

70

Surgeons and stewards at Harewood Hospital. *Library of Congress.*

Whitman responded to one such nurse, a Miss Gregg, in a letter that expressed his deep care for her:

> *You spoke the other day, partly in fun, about the men being so undemonstrative. I thought I would write you a line, as I hear you leave the hospital tomorrow for a few weeks. Your labor of love & disinterestedness here in Hospital is appreciated. I have invariably heard the Ward A patients speak of you with gratitude, sometimes with enthusiasm. They have their own ways (not outside eclat, but in manly American hearts, however rude, however undemonstrative to you). I thought it would be sweet to your tender & womanly heart, to know what I have so often heard from the soldiers about you, as I sat by their sick cots. I too have learnt to love you, seeing your tender heart, & your goodness to those wounded & dying young men—for they have grown to seem to me as my sons or dear young brothers.*[81]

He noted that one nurse, Washington native Rose Billing, "who has long been a practical friend of soldiers and nurse in the army, and had become attach'd to it in a way that no one can realize but him or her who has had experience, was taken sick, early this winter, linger'd some time, and finally died in the Hospital. It was her request that she should be buried among the soldiers, and after the military method." Billing had contracted typhoid at the general hospital of the U.S. Naval Academy in Annapolis and died in January 1865. Her wish was respected, and she was buried in Congressional Cemetery with a military escort.[82]

Whitman usually got along with the hospital staff—but not always. He got on the nerves of one nurse, Amanda Akin, who later wrote about her experience at Armory Square Hospital. Her tone came across as homophobic: "He took a fancy to my fever boy, and would watch with him sometimes half the night. He is a poet, and I believe has written some very queer books about 'Free Love,' etc…When he stalks down the ward I feel the 'prickings of my thumbs,' and never speak to him, if not obliged to do so…With all his peculiar interest in our soldier boys he does not appeal to me."[83]

The "fever boy" Akin wrote about was Erastus Haskell, a good-looking carpenter from Elmira, New York, who had come down with typhoid. Walt was clearly attached to the young soldier and spent many nights sitting by his side, fanning him in the heat. After Haskell died, Whitman scribbled down a heart-wrenching letter to Haskell's parents about the young man's final days.[84]

> *I write to you this letter, because I would do something at least in his memory—his fate was a hard one, to die so—He is one of the thousands of our unknown American young men in the ranks about whom there is no record or fame, no fuss made about their dying so unknown, but I find in them the real precious & royal ones of this land, giving themselves up, aye even their young & precious lives, in their country's cause.*[85]

Nurse Akin continued to maintain a low opinion about Walt. She wrote in her diary on November 12, 1863: "Read a very ludicrous and characteristic letter from Walt Whitman to his 'fellow comrades,' as he called the soldiers. And they failed to understand the jumbled sentences written on foolscap, they brought it to me. He was spending a vacation with his mother in Brooklyn, and his love for them was repeated in many incoherent sentences.

I could only imagine it was written very late at night and he had taken 'a drop too much.'"[86] Akin didn't like Whitman, but neither did he care for her. They were mutually cold to each other.

Another Armory Square nurse, Harriet Ward Foote Hawley of the U.S. Christian Commission, highly disapproved of Walt. She wrote to her husband, a general, in February 1865: "There comes that odious Walt Whitman to talk evil and unbelief to my boys. I think I would rather see the Evil One himself—at least if he had horns and hooves...I shall get him out as soon as possible."[87]

Once when Walt and Nelly O'Connor were walking down Fifteenth Street, "a woman passing drew herself far away, as if afraid of contamination by even a touch of his garment," Nelly wrote. Walt said, "'Oh yes, some persons feel that way towards me, and do not hide it.'"[88]

LOUISA MAY ALCOTT

One of the little-known facts about Washington during the Civil War was that author Louisa May Alcott worked as a nurse at the Union Hotel for six weeks in December 1862 and January 1863. Alcott was thirty years old and described herself as a spinster, which was not inaccurate for her time, given that women married early in the nineteenth century.

Alcott was raised in Concord, Massachusetts, home of transcendentalism and numerous writers, such as Ralph Waldo Emerson, Nathaniel Hawthorne and Henry David Thoreau. It was also a hotbed of

Author Louisa May Alcott briefly served as a nurse at the Union Hotel hospital. *Library of Congress.*

LOUISA M. ALCOTT,
THE AUTHOR OF "LITTLE WOMEN,"

abolitionism, and Alcott was a proud third-generation abolitionist. She had written and published numerous short stories, but she wasn't the literary giant yet as we know her; rather, she was barely scraping by financially, as she had to support her family. Her philosopher-teacher father, Branson Alcott, was near useless as a breadwinner. From reading her personal journals, it is clear that she continually worried about financial insecurity.

Women on both sides of the war knitted and sewed clothing for the soldiers, as clothing was still largely a cottage industry. Louisa May Alcott spent countless hours during the first two years of the war sewing. Finally, she decided to do more. In December 1862, she volunteered for a three-month stint as a hospital nurse in Washington. Alcott wrote in her journal: "I've often longed to see a war, and now I have my wish. I long to be a man, but as I can't fight, I will content myself with working for those who can."[89]

Alcott received permission to serve as a nurse from Dorothea Dix, the superintendent of female nurses in Washington. Dix was a quarrelsome woman, sixty years old at the start of the war and widely disliked by the surgeons and even by many of the nurses. Alcott called her "a kind soul but very queer & arbitrary."[90]

Alcott described her experiences in an autobiographical work called *Hospital Sketches*, though she gave herself the rather ridiculous pen name of Tribulation Periwinkle. She called Washington a "camp of hospitals."[91] Alcott had hoped to be stationed at Armory Square Hospital but instead was assigned to the Union Hotel Hospital, a temporary facility in Georgetown (M and Thirtieth Streets Northwest). She referred to it as "Hurly-burly House" for its distressful condition.[92] In her journal, Alcott described it as "a more perfect pestilence-box than this house I never saw—cold, damp, dirty, full of vile odors from wounds, kitchens, wash rooms, & stables. No competent head, male or female, to right matters, & a jumble of good, bad, & indifferent nurses, surgeons & attendants to complicate the Chaos still more."[93]

The first wounded that Alcott treated were from the Battle of Fredericksburg—the same battle that drew Walt Whitman to Washington. The wounded seemed to arrive all at once. "All was hurry and confusion; the hall was full of these wrecks of humanity," Alcott wrote.[94] She was tasked with washing the soldiers and then helped feed them. She changed bandages and wrote letters for the men. This first shift overwhelmed the inexperienced nurse.

My three days' experiences had begun with a death, and, owing to the defalcation of another nurse, a somewhat abrupt plunge into the superintendence of a ward containing forty beds, where I spend my shining hours washing faces, serving rations, giving medicine, and sitting in a very hard chair, with pneumonia on one side, diphtheria on the other, five typhoids on the opposite, and a dozen dilapidated patriots, hopping, lying, and lounging about, all staring more or less at the new "nuss," who suffered untold agonies, but concealed them under as matronly an aspect as a spinster could assume, and blundered through her trying labors with a Spartan firmness, which I hope they appreciated, but I am afraid they didn't.[95]

Alcott's prose could be achingly beautiful. She described the last moments of a soldier named John Suhre, a Union soldier and blacksmith from Virginia who was universally beloved in the hospital ward for his kind demeanor. He had been fatally shot through the lung.

He laid himself gently down; and, stretching out his strong right arm, as if to gasp and bring the blessed air to his lips in a fuller flow, lapsed into a merciful unconsciousness, which assured us that for him suffering was forever past. He died then; for, though the heavy breaths still tore their way up for a little longer, they were but the waves of an ebbing tide that beat unfelt against the wreck, which an immortal voyager had deserted with a smile.[96]

Alcott had volunteered for three months of nursing at ten dollars per month, but she served only six weeks, as she came down with typhoid, which she likely picked up in the hospital. When her condition failed to improve after several weeks, her father came to take her home to Concord in January 1863. Alcott was deathly ill. For three weeks, she was delirious with fever before her condition improved. The mercury-based medicine used to treat typhoid made her hair fall out. Alcott wrote in her journal: "Felt badly about losing my one beauty. Never mind, it might have been my head & a wig outside is better than a loss of wits inside."[97]

It is unlikely that Alcott and Whitman met. They both arrived in Washington in December 1862; he went to Fredericksburg to find his brother George while she worked at the Union Hotel hospital. And even if their paths crossed, would they have known each other? Alcott was not yet well known as a writer, and Whitman was still relatively obscure. Neither had reason to look for the other, though Whitman had met her father soon after publishing *Leaves of Grass*. Branson Alcott would have had no reason to suspect that Whitman was in Washington in early 1863. He was on a mission of mercy to rescue his daughter.

After recovering from typhoid, Alcott published *Hospital Sketches* in the spring of 1863. It was her first literary success, and after that, she began publishing novels and fictional stories more frequently. She is best known for *Little Women* (1868) and *Little Men* (1871), two of the most widely known novels about the Civil War.

CLARA BARTON'S MISSING SOLDIERS OFFICE

Another person who gained a national reputation during the Civil War was Clara Barton. Barton was hired to work in the Patent Office as a federal clerk in 1854, and she was the first woman to be paid equal to a man's salary at $1,500 a year. Some of the men blew cigar smoke at her and questioned her morality, but she persevered. She lost her job in 1857 when James Buchanan became president (all clerks were political appointments). She returned home to Massachusetts but only for a few years.

Barton was forty years old and unmarried when the Civil War broke out. When Abraham Lincoln was elected president, she was offered a job at the Patent Office again but not at her old pay. Still, she accepted the position in 1861 and sublet a room on the third floor of a boardinghouse at 488½ Seventh Street Northwest. She officially worked at the Patent Office for the next four years, though she spent little time there, hiring a substitute instead. She found a more important calling.

With Barton's return to Washington, she began gathering hospital supplies for the Union troops. She received a noncombatant pass to accompany the Army of the Potomac and made her first foray into the field in August 1862, encountering thousands of wounded men in the chaotic aftermath of the Second Battle of Bull Run. She and her teamsters followed the army, their wagons loaded with supplies. They were soon put to use at the Battle of Antietam, fought on September 17, 1862. It was the bloodiest day in American history, and she was nearly shot on the battlefield as she nursed a wounded man. The bullet killed the soldier before passing through her dress. That day, she earned her nickname: the Angel of the Battlefield.

A Civil War–era image of Clara Barton. *Library of Congress.*

Wherever the army went, Barton was near the front. She was tough, she brought relief and the soldiers came to love her. Even the higher-ranking army officers came to appreciate her cutting through red tape to bring much-needed supplies that could mean life or death for the soldiers. She stockpiled so many hospital goods that she rented two more adjacent rooms in the boardinghouse. Barton rejoined the army before the Battle of Fredericksburg, when she was yet again near the front, helping the wounded at the Lacy House. She was later appointed superintendent of nurses for the Union Army of the James.

As the war wound down, Barton transitioned from nursing and providing relief to helping find missing soldiers. As ships brought emaciated Union prisoners of war to Annapolis, Maryland, a general hospital was established on the grounds of the U.S. Naval Academy. Barton compiled a lengthy list and posted this in Annapolis. She was never asked to do this; she simply saw a need and took the initiative. Her efforts drew the attention of President Lincoln, who advertised in March 1865 that people should contact Barton for information about missing soldiers.

Barton converted her hospital supply storage in the Seventh Street boardinghouse into the Missing Soldiers Office, renting two additional rooms. She and her staff were soon inundated with letters from families inquiring about their missing brothers, fathers and sons—some sixty-two thousand soldiers. Barton and her assistants wrote 41,855 replies to these inquiries and helped locate more than twenty-one thousand missing men.

Clara Barton's Missing Soldiers Office was in the adjacent apartment in a Seventh Street Northwest boardinghouse. *Garrett Peck.*

After the war, Barton traveled to the Andersonville prison camp in Georgia to help identify the dead and missing and install grave markers for thirteen thousand graves. She journeyed there with Dorence Atwater, a Union soldier imprisoned there who had smuggled out the death list. Atwater was court-martialed for stealing the list back from the government, but Barton used her influence with President Andrew Johnson to have him pardoned. An appreciative Congress appropriated $15,000 after the fact for Barton's Andersonville project. It provided her the money to continue the Missing Soldiers Office, since she had been laid off from federal employment in the same sweep that cost Walt Whitman his job.[98]

In 1868, Barton wrapped up her work at the Missing Soldiers Office. She threw some belongings in the attic, closed the office and moved to Europe for several years. She later founded the American Red Cross and eventually moved to its headquarters and warehouse in Glen Echo, Maryland, where she died in 1912. The third floor of her old boardinghouse was boarded up a year later, and for 129 years, people forgot about Clara Barton's Missing Soldiers Office. The site was "lost" in part because the city realigned its addressing system in the 1870s. The boardinghouse became 437 Seventh Street Northwest.

By 1997, the federal General Services Agency (GSA) owned the building. The GSA hired a contractor, Richard Lyons, to prepare the building for demolition. Walking through Barton's old room, he saw a letter sticking out of the attic above him. Climbing a ladder to investigate, he found a veritable Clara Barton time capsule, untouched for more than a century: hundreds of socks, letters and a Missing Soldiers Office sign. The discovery saved the building from demolition. However, it took years to restore the building. The GSA mandated that the building be returned to its original boardinghouse appearance from Barton's day, and even the wallpaper was replicated from original patterns. Clara Barton's Missing Soldiers Office museum, run by the National Museum of Civil War Medicine, opened in 2014.

One of the lingering questions from the Civil War era was whether Clara Barton ever met Walt Whitman. The two humanitarians were intimately involved in relief work, but did their paths ever cross? Both worked at the Patent Office, though at different times, and both were in the Lacy House after the Battle of Fredericksburg. Sadly, there is no documentation to indicate whether they met. "They met temporarily in a painting in the Capitol," said Steve Livengood of the U.S. Capitol

Historical Society. "But then someone researched and found that Walt did not arrive in town until after they stopped using the Rotunda as a hospital—so they painted him out, and Clara sits alone, posing in front of the soldiers in the Cox Corridor painting."

Chapter 5

THE FIRST DISCIPLES

Whitman met two of the best friends he would ever have, William Douglas O'Connor and John Burroughs, while he lived in Washington. In fact, these two men would be more than friends; they are considered his first two disciples.[99]

Soon after arriving in Washington, Whitman bumped into William O'Connor. They had met in Boston in 1860, as they had shared the same publisher, Thayer & Eldridge. O'Connor and Charles Eldridge had provided Walt with emergency cash, and after Walt returned from Fredericksburg, O'Connor and his wife, Nelly, offered to let Whitman stay with them. Walt accepted. He rented a "bright little 3d story front room" at 394 L Street (now 1407 L Street Northwest) for seven dollars per month, including board. This helped the O'Connors defray their twenty-five-dollar monthly rent in the inflated wartime housing market.[100]

On New Year's Day 1863, O'Connor and Whitman visited the White House for the annual levee, but the crowds were so great that they didn't get to meet President Lincoln. The president shook thousands of hands, and then after his hand was exhausted and the last guest left, he carefully took up a pen to sign the Emancipation Proclamation. Several blocks away, O'Connor and Whitman were passing in front of the Willard Hotel when they encountered poet John Piatt, one of William's friends, who was himself headed to the White House. Piatt and Whitman would become good acquaintances though never close friends. Piatt would occasionally join the salon at the O'Connor residence, and both William and Walt

An 1855 photograph of William Douglas O'Connor, who would become Walt Whitman's first disciple and keenest ally. *Library of Congress.*

nursed John back to health when he was struck by typhoid in the spring of 1864.[101] After the failure of his novel *Harrington*, O'Connor had taken a position as a federal clerk at the Light House Board, an office job in the Treasury Department. He worked there for the rest of his life, choosing the safety of a government job (one that made him fairly miserable) over the thrill of a literary life. O'Connor became a bureaucrat, a might-have-been in American literature. No doubt his wife, Nelly, had a hand in his career choice; she was a loving but cautious individual who stifled his ambitions. Their niece Grace Channing recalled how much Nelly had held William back. She described her aunt as

an exceptional and extraordinary woman, and the very last a man of imagination or genius should have married. It is enough to say of her that while she made an incomparable hostess and was the understanding friend of all the brilliant circle which nightly adorned her house, her conscientious attitude towards life, as it affected her, was that one should not give up a certainty for an uncertainty. She was expressly and particularly framed to see life from the opposite standpoint of O'Connor and to quietly and unviolently frustrate every attempt of his native talent. She was the best stifler of self-expression in others I have ever known. Against the calm rock of her opposition, the great waves of his aspirations beat in vain. They ought to have separated as quickly as possible.[102]

William and Nelly O'Connor's marriage was a strained one (they had two children, one of whom died in 1862), and each devoted his or her affections to Walt in what seemed like a love triangle. Nelly, in fact, fell in love with Walt, a feeling that was not reciprocated, though Walt did consider her a dear friend. She sent him a number of love letters over the years, including one from Providence, Rhode Island, in November 1870 that declared: "I always know that you know that I love you all the time, even though we should never meet again, my feeling could never change, and I am *sure* that you know it as well as I do."[103] The fact was that Nelly and William loved having Walt around, and he was a welcome distraction to their strained relationship.

In the mornings, Walt dressed and sang. While Nelly O'Connor made breakfast, Walt's task was to fetch water. The house had no plumbing, so he walked to the corner pump carrying a pitcher, which he filled with cold water. "He was especially fond of taking a long draught of the same at the pump," Nelly remembered.[104] She described Walt as having an "elusive disposition" and a "dislike to be[ing] bound in any way." Soon after Walt arrived in Washington, his friend William Swinton dropped by the O'Connors'. Nelly recalled the conversation more than four decades later: "Well Walt, I have known you dozens of years, and made hundreds of appointments with you, but this is the first time that I ever knew you to keep one. I *thought* I saw signs of decay!"[105]

William O'Connor was Walt's best friend, and the two were often verbal sparring partners. Walt enjoyed taking long walks into the country, and the O'Connors occasionally joined him, venturing to the Navy Yard and across the Eastern Branch. Nelly recalled, "Sometimes we all went after dinner, when the days were longer, into the woods of Georgetown, and spent hours watching the rising moon, and the attractive landscape."[106]

Whitman made another lifelong friend in November 1863 when he met John Burroughs. Burroughs had recently moved to Washington without his wife, Ursula, and wanted to meet Walt. He heard that the poet was now living in the capital. It was a pilgrimage of sorts: Burroughs practically worshipped at the Whitman altar since first reading *Leaves of Grass* in 1860. He was already a gifted naturalist and writer.

Burroughs's first residence was a cot in Clapp and Company, an army goods store where his friend Elijah Allen worked (the store stood on E Street Northwest near Tenth Street and Ford's Theatre). Burroughs took a job as part of a grave-digging detail, a job that literally made him sick, but later found an unchallenging clerk's position at the Treasury Department's Currency Bureau in January 1864.

Elijah Allen was a mutual friend of Whitman's and Burroughs's, and Walt often bought supplies for his hospital visits at the store. Allen had written to Burroughs earlier, telling him all about Walt, whom Allen called the "Old Goat," and that the two were occasional drinking buddies. "Walt and I quaffed beer today from great goblets that would become the halls of Walhalla," Allen bragged in a letter to Burroughs. "Walt is much interested in you, and I sketched your history some to him."[107]

Burroughs hung around Clapp and Company, waiting for Whitman to appear. At last, one evening, Burroughs entered the store and found Walt was already there, sitting in a camp chair. Allen introduced them. Burroughs was twenty-six years old, and Walt was forty-four. Impressed with Burroughs's intelligence and his keen knowledge of nature, Whitman later told Allen, "His face is like a field of wheat."[108]

Burroughs and Whitman met several more times at the store. One Sunday, Burroughs ran into Walt, who was en route to a hospital with his haversack full of supplies. Walt spontaneously invited Burroughs to join him, and Burroughs accepted. It was this hospital visit that helped solidify their friendship. John was a confirmed heterosexual, but Walt undoubtedly took a fancy to his young lettered comrade. Just a month after meeting Whitman, Burroughs confessed to a friend, "I have been much with Walt. Have even slept with him. I love him very much. The more I see and talk with him, the greater he becomes to me." The phrase "have even slept with him" isn't necessarily taken in a sexual sense: they simply shared a bed one night. But it was clear that John had a "man crush"—if you will—on Walt.[109]

In January 1864, Burroughs fairly gushed to that same friend: "He loves everything and everybody. I saw a soldier the other day stop on the street and kiss him. He kisses me as if I were a girl. He appreciates everybody, and no soul will get fuller justice in the next world than it gets at his hands here." He added, "He bathed today while I was there—such a handsome body, and such delicate, rosy flesh I never saw before. I told him he looked good enough to eat, which, he said, he should consider a poor recommendation if he were among the cannibals."[110] Had Burroughs been gay, he might have been an ideal match for Walt, but they developed a friendship that would last the rest of Whitman's life.

Both Burroughs and Whitman enjoyed nature, long walks and conversations that went on for hours. They often hiked along Rock Creek and Piney Branch, which was possibly where Burroughs, an expert ornithologist, pointed out the shy thrush, a bird that would figure prominently in Whitman's poems. Burroughs was known to foray as far as Cabin John, the site of the newly completed Union Arch aqueduct (Cabin John Bridge).

During one of their walks near the Capitol, they came upon a dirty and disheveled-looking soldier. Walt kindly stopped the young man. "I shall never forget how the soldier altered the tone in which he was answering him, as he looked Walt in the face," Burroughs remembered. "The soldier looked down at his boots and began to be ashamed of his appearance, since here was some one who took an interest in him." Burroughs continued:

> *Walt, in his tender, curious way, asked him if he should not help him a little—not enough to hurt him, but enough to get him a bit of food, for he looked hungry. The soldier did not know how to meet this charge and came near breaking down outright; and as Walt placed some small notes in his hand and turned away, he found his tongue to say, in that awkward, constrained way, that he hoped he would have good health and keep well. I saw how deeply he responded to this act of kindness, and how poorly his words expressed what he felt.*

Whitman wasn't naïve about the soldier, but that didn't seem to matter. "Walt said he had probably been guilty of some misdemeanor, perhaps was a deserter, or a returning rebel," Burroughs wrote. "But I saw that this incident would do more to strengthen and encourage him, and help restore his lost manhood, if so it was, then [*sic*] all the sermons and homilies and tracts that have ever been preached or printed."[111]

The President and the Poet

Whitman was initially indifferent to President Abraham Lincoln, but as the Civil War pressed on, he came to appreciate and love him, even though the two men probably never met. Whitman admired the president from afar. Lincoln himself may have heard of Whitman, as there is some evidence that he read the 1856 edition of *Leaves of Grass* while he was a practicing attorney in Illinois.[112]

Lincoln was constantly besieged in the White House with crowds demanding his time and job-seekers looking for favors. In the summertime, Washington was sweltering hot. Fortunately, he found a place of refuge in a spacious cottage at the Soldiers' Home. It stood in the quiet country three miles north of the White House. The Soldiers' Home was established in

Abraham Lincoln spent a quarter of his presidency in this cottage at the Soldiers' Home, three miles north of the White House. President Lincoln's Cottage opened to the public in 2008 and is today administered through the National Trust for Historic Preservation. *Garrett Peck.*

1851 as a retirement home for enlisted veterans, and about two hundred men, mostly German and Irish immigrants who had served in the U.S. military, lived there at the time of the Civil War. Even here, Lincoln couldn't escape the war: the cabinet often met in the cottage, and adjacent to the ground was a cemetery where details were busily digging graves. Lincoln was always reminded of the high cost of the war.

Lincoln spent an estimated quarter of his presidency at the cottage, and there he drafted the Emancipation Proclamation and presented it to his cabinet. He often rode out to the cottage in the evening to stay the night and then returned to the White House the next morning. A cavalry detail escorted the president during his commute.

Whitman often saw Lincoln riding to or returning from the cottage at the Soldiers' Home. For part of 1863, Whitman was living with the O'Connors at 394 L Street North (now 1100 Vermont Avenue Northwest). Whitman wrote in the *New York Times* on August 16: "I see the President almost every day, as I happen to live where he passes to or from his lodgings out of town." Whitman noted that he was always accompanied by a cavalry detail, but it was Lincoln's appearance that made the biggest impression on him. "Mr. LINCOLN generally rides a good-sized easy-going gray horse, is dressed in plain black, somewhat rusty and dusty; wears a black stiff hat, and looks about as ordinary in attire, &c., as the commonest man...I saw very plainly the President's dark brown face, with the deep cut lines, the eyes, &c., always to me with a deep latent sadness in the expression." Whitman quoted the article in *Memoranda*, adding the well-known line: "We have got so that we always exchange bows, and very cordial ones."[113]

Lincoln's sad expression was partly from grief and worry, but it was also from exhaustion: the president faced chronic insomnia, and he was known to pace many sleepless nights through the cottage and White House as he pondered the Union's fate. Whitman added, "None of the artists or pictures have caught the deep, though subtle and indirect expression of this man's face. There is something else there. One of the great portrait painters of two or three centuries ago is needed."[114]

Whitman's friend and devotee William Douglas O'Connor related a possibly apocryphal story about Lincoln. One day, Lincoln looked out from a window in the White House and saw Whitman walking by. "Well, *he* looks like a Man!" the president supposedly remarked.[115]

On October 29, 1863, Whitman went to the White House to get a free train pass to New York from one of Lincoln's secretaries, John Hay, an acquaintance of William O'Connor's. Hay recorded in his diary, "Whitman the poet who is going to New York to electioneer and vote for the Union ticket."[116] (Walt noted the date as October 31.) Whitman saw Lincoln, but the

Abraham Lincoln in February 1865, photographed by Alexander Gardner. The president's face shows the heavy toll that the war had taken on him. *Library of Congress.*

Alfred Waugh sketched President Abraham Lincoln resting in a chair. *Library of Congress.*

president was having a private conversation. Walt departed without having met or spoken to Lincoln. He wrote in a notebook that Lincoln's "face & manner have an expression & are inexpressibly sweet—one hand on his friends [*sic*] shoulder the other holding his hand. I love the President personally."[117]

Chapter 6
HOSPITAL MALARIA

After ten months in Washington, Whitman returned to Brooklyn on November 2, 1863, on a much-needed break—and to vote in the local election. He was elated that Brooklyn supported the president and elected a slate of pro-Union candidates. He addressed a letter to Lewy Brown, but it was really written for all the soldiers he had befriended in Armory Square Hospital. In it, he sent his love and named many of the soldiers and nurses. (This was the same letter to which Nurse Akin had taken offense for having to read aloud.) Walt was excited to be home and realized how life in New York just went on, almost oblivious to the war. "Well, dear comrades, it looks so different here in all this mighty city, every thing going with a big rush & so gay, as if there was neither war nor hospitals in the land. New York & Brooklyn appear nothing but prosperity & plenty," he wrote. Walt went to the opera, caught up with friends and went to many dinner parties. He wrote poetry for his planned book *Drum-Taps*. For a month, Walt was a bohemian again.[118]

When the war started, Whitman began writing poems that would eventually become *Drum-Taps*. He envisioned publishing the book as early as 1863 and wrote many of the poems while living in Washington. He also considered publishing a book—which would become *Memoranda of a Year*—about his 1863 experiences, but he never brought it out.[119]

Whitman returned to Washington in early December and immediately received a telegram announcing his brother Andrew's death from consumption. Walt did not go back to Brooklyn for the funeral. He resumed

A signed 1864 carte de visite of Walt Whitman, taken by Alexander Gardner. *Library of Congress.*

his hospital visits and made another appeal for a federal position, this time in the Treasury Department with the help of novelist John Trowbridge. Trowbridge had been hired to write treasury secretary Salmon Chase's biography for the upcoming 1864 presidential campaign, and thus, he was staying as a guest in Chase's mansion in November and December 1863. He was friends with William O'Connor, who invited him over to see Walt. "On seeing him again at O'Connor's, I found Whitman had little changed, except that he was more trimly attired, wearing a loosely fitting but quite elegant suit of black,—yes, black at last!" Trowbridge wrote. After dinner, O'Connor, Trowbridge and Whitman made their way to Walt's garret apartment at 415 Sixth Street.

Diagonally opposite to Chase's great house, on the corner of E and 6th streets, stood one of those old wooden buildings which then and for some years afterwards lingered among the new and handsome blocks rising around them, and made the "city of magnificent distances" also a city of astonishing architectural contrasts. In the fine, large mansion, sumptuously furnished, cared for by sleek and silent colored servants, and thronged by distinguished guests, dwelt the great states man; in the old tenement opposite, in a bare and desolate back room, up three flights of stairs, quite alone, lived the poet. Walt led the way up those dreary stairs, partly in darkness, found the key hole of a door which he unlocked and opened, scratched a match, and welcomed us to his garret.

Garret it literally was, containing hardly any more furniture than a bed, a cheap pine table, and a little sheet-iron stove in which there was no fire. A window was open, and it was a December night. But Walt, clearing a chair or two of their litter of newspapers, invited us to sit down and stop awhile, with as simple and sweet hospitality as if he had been offering us the luxuries of the great mansion across the street.

The three writers spent the rest of the evening discussing Shakespeare and *Leaves of Grass*. Trowbridge wrote of Whitman: "Ordinarily inert and slow of speech, on occasions like this his large and generous nature became suffused with a magnificent glow, which gave one some idea of the heat and momentum that went to the making of his truly great poems."[120]

When Trowbridge learned that Whitman had a letter of recommendation from Ralph Waldo Emerson—one of the three that Emerson had written a year earlier—Trowbridge agreed to present it to the treasury secretary. Chase was well aware that Whitman was the famous (and infamous) author of *Leaves of Grass* and immediately objected to hiring him as he was a disreputable person. However, Chase was a signature collector. "I have nothing of Emerson's in his handwriting, and I shall be glad to keep this," he told Trowbridge. He kept the letter.

When Whitman learned later that day of what happened, he replied sardonically, "He is right in preserving his saints from contamination by a man like me!"[121] Chase later changed his mind, and realizing that the Emerson letter was official government business, he turned it over to the National Archives.

Walt continued working at the Army Paymaster Office, writing freelance articles and fundraising. In February 1864, he journeyed to the Union army camp at Culpeper, Virginia, with the paymaster and his assistant, Major Lyman Hapgood and Charles Eldridge. They were paying out reenlistment bonuses to the Army of the Potomac. Walt described Virginia, once a bountiful state, as "dilapidated, fenceless, and trodden with war." His brother George wasn't in camp, being instead in Brooklyn on furlough.[122]

THE WAR IN 1864

In the spring of 1864, the third year of the Civil War, the Union marshaled its forces for a knockout blow to the Confederacy. Ulysses S. Grant was appointed general in chief and prepared mighty offensives to strike at the Confederate armies. George Whitman, whose regiment had spent the past year campaigning in Tennessee and against Vicksburg, was sent to reinforce the Union Army of the Potomac for the great offensive against Richmond known as the Overland Campaign.

On April 25, 1864, Whitman and John Burroughs watched the Ninth Corps parade through Washington for more than three hours on its way to the front. Despite the crowd—some thirty thousand Union soldiers were parading through the city—Walt waded right into the ranks to find George when the Fifty-first New York marched passed. He wrote to their mother the next day about the excitement of seeing his brother: "I joined him just before they came to where the President & Gen Burnside were standing with others on a balcony, & the interest of seeing me &c. made George forget to notice the President & salute him—he was a little annoyed at forgetting it."

In that same letter, Whitman observed how Lincoln had respectfully removed his hat for the soldiers marching passed—even for the black soldiers, who were a growing part of the Union army. Walt found that odd. "There were I should think five very full regiments of new black troops under Gen Ferrero, they looked & marched very well—It looked funny to see the President standing with his hat off to them just the same as the rest as they passed by."[123]

Yet Walt could also admire African Americans, at least when it came to same-sex attraction. Nelly O'Connor recalled that Walt wandered over to Georgetown and happened upon a C&O Canal barge that was offloading coal. "He watched for hours a negro at work, who was naked to the waist, and the play of his muscles, as he loaded and unloaded the buckets of coal, was most fascinating: 'No Greek statue could have been more superb,' he said."[124]

ARLINGTON NATIONAL CEMETERY

In May 1864, the Union armies began their springtime offensive against the Confederacy. The Union Army of the Potomac moved against Robert E. Lee's Army of Northern Virginia in a series of brutal clashes as Ulysses Grant sought to take Richmond. The Wilderness, Spotsylvania and Cold Harbor were the first of the battles that inflicted enormous casualties before the armies settled down for the siege of Petersburg. The wounded flooded into Washington by the thousands. Many died from their wounds.

The Civil War created a significant new problem for the capital city: where to bury the thousands of dead? There were numerous cemeteries in the city, but none was large enough to handle the vast number of casualties. Congressional Cemetery on Capitol Hill was the first national burial ground, but it was too small. Other cemeteries sprouted up—such as at the Soldiers' Home near the Lincoln cottage, as well as Alexandria National Cemetery—but these were quickly filling up. By the spring of 1864, Quartermaster General Montgomery Meigs needed to find a new resting place for the Union dead. He searched for a consolidated location that would be spacious enough for tens of thousands of burials.

One day in May 1864, Meigs was on a carriage ride with President Lincoln, and the two crossed the Potomac River to visit a field hospital on the grounds of Arlington House, Robert E. Lee's mansion and plantation. Meigs realized that this estate was just over the river from the city's many hospitals—and that its large open space could be the resting spot that he needed. He ordered the first burials on Lee's property that day. On June 15, Secretary of War Edwin Stanton signed the order establishing the Lee plantation as a military cemetery. Arlington National Cemetery was born. By the end of the war, some five thousand Union dead were interred there. Many more would follow.[125]

One of the first soldiers to be buried at Arlington was a young man whom Whitman had worked long to help. Walt had taken a liking to Oscar Cunningham, a strapping twenty-year-old soldier from Ohio whom he met in Armory Square Hospital. "I though he ought to have been taken by a sculptor to model for an emblematical figure of the west, he was such a handsome young giant, over 6 feet high, a great head of brown yellowy shining hair thick & longish & a manly noble manner & talk," Walt wrote in a notebook.[126] Cunningham had badly fractured his right leg above the knee at the Battle of Chancellorsville in May 1863, and the wound would not heal. He suffered greatly, the young man wasting away over the next year, though the doctors worked hard to save his leg. A year after being wounded, the surgeons decided to amputate the leg. It was too late. Cunningham declined until he was all but a skeleton. After thirteen months in the hospital, he succumbed on June 4, 1864.[127]

Walt exchanged letters with Cunningham's sister Helen during Oscar's last month, when he was too weak to write.[128] Oscar's death probably influenced Walt's poem "Come Up from the Fields Father," a heartbreaking poem about the news of a son's death delivered by letter. Though the poem names the dead soldier as "Pete"—and some assume this is Peter Doyle—it is more than likely referring to Oscar.[129]

Oscar Cunningham was a friend of Walt Whitman and one of the first Union soldiers to be buried at Arlington National Cemetery, in Section 27, Site 553. *Garrett Peck.*

Cunningham was buried in Arlington in Section 27, a section filled with the Union dead from 1864. A larger portion than expected is simply marked "Unknown." Cunningham's grave can be found at Site 553, right against the Seneca sandstone boundary wall that encircles the cemetery and within a stone's throw from the Netherlands Carillon. Whether Walt attended Cunningham's funeral isn't known. The record indicates that Whitman attended only three funerals during his decade in the district: those of Count Gurowski, Francis Doyle and his mother, Louisa. Walt seemed more concerned with the living and always had a long list of wounded soldiers to support. Going to funerals for several thousand soldiers may have simply been too much. He did, however, often write to the deceased's relatives.

WALT FALLS ILL

In the spring of 1864, Walt wrote in a notebook: "My opinion is *to stop the war now.*"[130] Nelly O'Connor remembered him railing at a Unitarian minister who supported the war, saying, "I say stop this war, this horrible massacre of men."[131] Walt remained a firm supporter of the Union, but he was overwhelmed by the war's human cost.

As the fighting intensified in Virginia, the casualties spiked, and the wounded arrived in droves in Washington. Walt wrote to his mother on May 25: "Mother, it is just the same old story, poor suffering young men, great swarms of them come up here, now, every day, all battered & bloody—there have 4000 arrived here this morning, & 1500 yesterday."[132] Meanwhile, Walt himself was suffering; he complained to his mother in several letters about headaches, which he initially thought were from the heat.[133]

Still, he trudged on with his hospital visits, though each letter home revealed his increasing desperation and his emotionally fragile state. He reckoned that a wounded soldier was dying every hour in the wards. Amid all this sadness, he tried to keep cheerful, as he wrote to his mother on June 3: "O, I must tell you I gave the boys in Carver hospital a great treat of ice cream a couple days ago. Went round myself through about 15 large wards (I bought some ten gallons, very nice)—you would have cried and been amused too, many of the men had to be fed, several of them I saw cannot probably live, yet they quite enjoyed it."[134]

The fighting was intense and protracted, the two armies digging siege lines and the men under constant fire and bombardment. "One new feature is that many of the poor afflicted young men are crazy, every ward has some in it that are wandering—they have suffered too much, & it is perhaps a privilege that they are out of their senses," Walt wrote, having witnessed a greater number of men who were suffering from post-traumatic stress disorder (PTSD).[135]

Whitman's health was breaking. He complained of fainting spells, headaches and a continuous sore throat. He became so sick—mentally, physically or both—that doctors told him he should leave Washington to recover. Walt persevered for another two weeks. On June 17, he wrote to his mother that he was finally returning to Brooklyn. He had sacrificed much—including his health—for the sick and the wounded.[136]

Walt was probably too ill to take notice of a tragedy that occurred that same day: the Washington Arsenal explosion. Twenty-one women, largely Irish immigrants, were killed and dozens more horribly injured and burned. President Lincoln attended the funeral at Congressional Cemetery as the entire city mourned.

Walt blamed his illness on "hospital malaria," a supposed virus that he ingested during his visits. More likely, Walt's medical condition suggests symptoms of hypertension combined with another ailment, such as a sinus or staph infection that he could have picked up from a sick patient. Whitman departed Washington for Brooklyn on June 23. As soon as he got to his mother's house, he took to bed for two weeks.

Whitman missed one of the most exciting events in Civil War Washington: Jubal Early's Raid and the Battle of Fort Stevens on July 11–12, 1864. All of the able-bodied men in the city were called up and armed to repel the Confederate attack, including federal clerks like John Burroughs and William O'Connor. Burroughs mentioned this fact in a letter to Walt: "I was out at the front during the *siege of Washington* and lay in the rifle pits with the soldiers. I got quite a taste of war and learned the song of those modern minstrels—the minnie [*sic*] bullets—by heart."[137]

Back in Brooklyn, Walt slowly recovered from his sickness and then resumed visiting the wounded in local hospitals. He also had to make a difficult family decision, committing his increasingly crazed older brother Jesse to an insane asylum. Jesse died there in 1870.

With more free time on his hands, Walt collected his thoughts about his wartime experiences. He drafted a six-thousand-word article, "Our Wounded and Sick Soldiers," for the *New York Times*, providing many details from his two years of hospital service. It ran on December 11, 1864. He based the article on the dozens of notebooks that he had kept, notes that he called "memoranda." It was this lengthy article, more than any other, that formed the basis for his 1876 book *Memoranda During the War*. He also continued composing poems for his next publication, a slim book that he called *Drum-Taps*.[138]

Walt might have remained in Brooklyn for good, but his sojourn lasted only seven months. He would unexpectedly return to Washington in January 1865 with an offer of federal employment.

Chapter 7
OF A YOUTH WHO LOVES ME

*Of a youth who loves me and whom I love, silently
approaching and seating himself near, that he may hold
me by the hand,
A long while, amid the noises of coming and going, of
drinking and oath and smutty jest,
There we two, content, happy in being together, speaking
little, perhaps not a word.*

– *"A Glimpse," from "Calamus,"* Leaves of Grass, *1860*

It is largely a settled question that Walt Whitman was gay. Only it wasn't called "gay" in his time—that word simply meant happy and merry. Even the term homosexual wasn't invented until 1892, the year of Whitman's death. The cultural vocabulary for homosexuality was not far advanced, though there were code words, such as "comrades."

We know of Whitman's sexual orientation largely through his letters to objects of interest, interviews with people who knew him and his poetry. He had a romantic relationship with Fred Vaughan in 1858 and 1859 that ended badly but led to his writing the homoerotic "Calamus" poems, which were published in the third (1860) edition of *Leaves of Grass*.

The soldiers Walt met in the hospital wards must have provided every sort of temptation for him, given that he was attracted to young farmhands and working-class men. And given the youth of the Union army, he had many opportunities to find fellow travelers. Whitman historian Daniel Mark Epstein concluded, "Whether he wanted to or not, in the intoxication of that first year in the hospitals he lost his perspective—he began to interpret certain soldiers' craving for attention as romantic love."[139]

Whitman developed crushes on Lewy Brown and Thomas Sawyer, two soldiers he met in the hospital, and became especially infatuated with Sawyer. Tom was possibly a case of unrequited love. As the soldier prepared to return to his army unit, Walt prepared a farewell gift of clothing, but Sawyer skipped town. Walt was clearly hurt, as he wrote to Tom:

> *I was sorry you did not come up to my room to get the shirt & other things you promised to accept from me and take when you went away. I got them all ready, a good strong blue shirt, a pair of drawers & socks, and it would have been a satisfaction to me if you had accepted them. I should have often thought now Tom may be wearing around his body something from me, & that it might contribute to your comfort, down there in camp on picket, or sleeping in your tent.*[140]

Sawyer possibly wanted to avoid the awkward situation of being in Whitman's bedroom alone with him. Walt continued to write for months, and Sawyer continued to not write back. Whitman ached. He had invested too much in pursuing someone who wasn't interested in him. Sawyer later married and had eight children.

One soldier with whom Whitman clearly had sexual relations was Alonzo Bush, an Indiana cavalryman and friend of Lewy Brown's who was likewise hospitalized at Armory Square. Bush wrote to Whitman a sexually explicit (if grammatically awkward) letter, hinting at their having had a threesome with Brown: "The fellow that went down on your BK, both So often with me. I wished that I could See him this evening and go in the Ward Master's Room and have Some fun for he is a gay boy." It is tempting to put a modern spin on Bush's use of "gay boy," but he simply meant that Brown was a fun playmate. And Bush was just that to Walt: a playmate.[141]

It was in a young Irishman, however, that Walt finally met his match.

Peter Doyle was born in Limerick, Ireland, on June 3, 1843, the son of Peter Doyle Sr. and Catherine Nash Doyle. He came to the United States in 1852 as an eight-year-old in an era of mass emigration for the Irish, who fled poverty and the potato famine. His family initially moved to Alexandria, Virginia, where they attended St. Mary's Catholic Church, but with the

The Old Capitol Prison is now the site of the U.S. Supreme Court. Peter Doyle was imprisoned for a month in 1863 in the Carroll Prison annex. *Library of Congress.*

economic downturn of 1856–57, they moved to Richmond, as Pete's father found a job at the Tredegar Iron Works.[142]

When the Civil War began, teenaged Pete enlisted in the Confederate army. He fought in many major engagements with the Army of Northern Virginia in the first seventeen months of the war and then was wounded at the Battle of Antietam. At that point, Pete decided it was time to leave the army while he was still alive.

Pete swore an affidavit that he was an Irish citizen, not a citizen of the Confederacy; that he had no family in the Confederacy (patently untrue, since his parents and siblings lived in Richmond); and that he intended to return to Ireland. Pete was discharged from Confederate service on November 7, 1862. Yet the young man remained in Richmond until he was arrested in the spring of 1863. He finally decided to leave Virginia rather than risk being drafted back into the army. Pete escaped north to Washington but was captured by

Union forces. He was imprisoned for a month at the Carroll Prison annex to the Old Capitol Prison and then was released on May 11, 1863.

Doyle initially moved in with his elder brother Francis's family in Southwest. He took several jobs: first as a blacksmith at the Navy Yard during the day (December 1863 to June 1865) and then as a horsecar conductor for the Washington and Georgetown Railroad. Since the streetcar terminated right at the Navy Yard, it was easy for him to jump right into his second job, and it was close to his home.

Pete later set up residence with his mother and two siblings. He was the main breadwinner for the household. In the 1871 city directory, he was listed

Beginning in 1862, a horsecar (streetcar) line connected Navy Yard to Georgetown, and the tracks ran around the Capitol. This photograph shows the east front of the building, taken near John Burroughs's house. *Historical Society of Washington, D.C.*

as a conductor living at M Street near Fourth and a Half Street Southwest. This was in the working-class neighborhood of the "Island," what we call today the Waterfront.

One wintry night in 1865, Whitman was returning from a meeting at John Burroughs's house on Capitol Hill when he jumped on the horsecar to get home. He found the car empty and sat down on a bench. It was a cold and stormy night, and the car was unheated, its only light source a single oil lamp that hung from the ceiling. Walt wore a blanket around his coat to keep warm. Pete noticed him right away. Perhaps they had exchanged a knowing glance when Walt entered the horsecar, but it was Pete who made the first move.

Decades later, Doyle related the story of how he met Whitman to two of Walt's literary executors, Maurice Bucke and Horace Traubel. Bucke went on to publish the story—along with Whitman's correspondence to Doyle—in 1897. Pete explained:

> *You ask where I first met him? It is a curious story. We felt to each other at once. I was a conductor. The night was very stormy,—he had been over to see [John] Burroughs before he came down to take the car—the storm was awful. Walt had his blanket—it was thrown round his shoulders—he seemed like an old sea-captain. He was the only passenger, it was a lonely night, so I thought I would go in and talk with him. Something in me made me do it and something in him drew me that way. He used to say there was something in me had the same effect on him. Anyway, I went into the car. We were familiar at once—I put my hand on his knee—we understood. He did not get out at the end of the trip—in fact went all the way back with me...From that time on we were the biggest sort of friends.*[143]

Thus began a relationship that lasted more than twenty-seven years, until Whitman's death in 1892. Doyle and Whitman became lovers or, in more modern parlance, partners.

What did they see in each other? At forty-five, Whitman was more than twice Doyle's age (twenty-one years), and yet the attraction was instant. Whitman was one of America's great poets, though Doyle had no idea about that. Doyle was young, but despite his youth, grammar school education and humble station, he had seen enough adventures for several lifetimes. He was charming, full of youthful and working-class vigor (always an attraction for Walt) and quick to laugh and smile. Both men had seen the gruesome effects of the battlefield and knew the tragic nature of war. Pete may have embodied the class of Manhattan stage drivers to whom Walt had devoted his attentions, cares and desires.

Whitman was six feet tall, a bit on the heavy side, with a big gray beard—he would be called a "bear" in the gay community today. Doyle was slight and four inches shorter than Walt. They were on the opposite sides of the Civil War: Pete a Confederate, Walt a Unionist. But the parallels in their lives were uncanny. Like Whitman, Doyle was one of eight children. Like Walt, he was a breadwinner for the family after his father died. And like Walt, he was named after his father. Their birthdays were a week apart. The poet and the conductor were soon inseparable. Pete and Walt were enormously good for each other. Doyle was Whitman's longest romantic relationship, even though the two never lived together.

Peter Doyle's biographer Martin Murray called Pete the "poet's muse." But how much influence did Pete have on Walt's poetry, such as the 1865 publication of *Drum-Taps* or subsequent editions of *Leaves of Grass*? We can't be certain. Some credit Pete's witnessing Lincoln's assassination as inspiring Walt to write "O Captain! My Captain!" and "When Lilacs Last in the Dooryard Bloom'd." Whitman's famous "Death of Abraham Lincoln" speech, which he started giving in 1879, was based on Pete's eyewitness account of Lincoln's assassination.[144]

Whitman began hanging out with Pete more and more, often joining him during his horsecar shift. Pete often dropped by Walt's office and got acquainted with many of Whitman's fellow clerks. "Walt rode with me often—often at noon, always at night. He rode round with me on the last trip—sometimes rode for several trips. Everybody knew him," Pete said. "He had a way of taking the measure of the driver's hands—had calf-skin gloves made for them every winter in Georgetown—these gloves were his personal presents to the men."[145]

After work, Doyle and Whitman often got a table in the Union Hotel in Georgetown, near the end of the horsecar line (coincidentally, in the same hotel where Louisa May Alcott had volunteered as a nurse). Doyle recalled their evenings together: "It was our practice to go to a hotel on Washington Avenue [now M Street Northwest] after I was done with my car. I remember the place well—there on the corner. Like as not I would go to sleep—lay my head on my hands on the table. Walt would sit there, wait, watch, keep me undisturbed—would wake me up when the hour of closing came."[146]

Whitman was enormously patient. He had sat at the bedside of many a dying young man; he let Pete sleep at the table, never concerned if he was wasting his time on a late evening date. He knew that Doyle initially worked two jobs to support his mother and younger siblings and that he was

Walt Whitman and Peter Doyle. Above the photograph is inscribed, "Washington D.C. 1865—Walt Whitman and his rebel soldier friend Pete Doyle." *Library of Congress.*

exhausted. Pete worked in the low-wage sector—it took two jobs to survive in wartime Washington. Whitman made more money as a federal clerk, putting him solidly in the middle class. An open question is where they spent their nights together: at Pete's or at Walt's.

When they had a day off from work, Pete and Walt would take enormous, daylong hikes around the Washington area, just as Walt had

The Union Hotel in Georgetown (M Street at Thirtieth Street Northwest) is where Louisa May Alcott served as a volunteer nurse and where Walt Whitman met Peter Doyle at the end of Doyle's streetcar shifts. The building was razed in 1935. *Library of Congress.*

done with John Burroughs. "We would walk together for miles and miles, never sated. Often we would go on for some time without a word, then talk—Pete a rod ahead or I a rod ahead," Walt said. "It was a great, a precious, a memorable experience."[147] Pete had similar fond memories of their walks: "We took great walks together—off towards or to Alexandria, often. We went plodding along the road, Walt always whistling or singing. We would talk of ordinary matters. He would recite poetry, especially Shakespeare—he would hum airs or shout in the woods. He was always active, happy, cheerful, good-natured. Many of our walks were taken at night. He never seemed to tire."

A favorite hike crossed the Anacostia River via the Navy Yard Bridge and trekked to the Alexandria ferry. They would cross the Potomac and then follow the Alexandria Canal or the railroad tracks north to the Long Bridge, where they'd return to Washington. This was a considerable distance. It must have been quite pleasant to get out of the noxious, dusty city and walk among the trees and streams—and along the majestic Potomac River. These walks must have been pleasant and invigorating for both men, as well as exhausting.[148]

Walt and Pete enjoyed simple pleasures. Pete described a favorite: "We would tackle the farmers who came into town, buy a watermelon, sit down on the cellar door of Bacon's grocery [at Center Market], Seventh & Pennsylvania Avenue, halve it and eat it. People would go by and laugh. Walt would only smile and say, 'They can have the laugh—we have the melon.'"[149]

Walt was always disposed toward personal acts of charity, a habit that Pete keenly observed (and sometimes contested, especially when it came to beggars). Pete's response seems timeless: it raises a question that we still face today, of whether we should give money directly to the homeless.

> *He always had a few pennies for beggars along the street. I'd get out of patience sometimes, he was so lenient. "Don't you think its wrong?" I'd ask him. "No," he always said—"it's never wrong, Peter." Wouldn't they drink it away? He shook his head: "No, and if they did it wouldn't alter the matter. For it is better to give to a dozen who do not need what is given than to give to none at all and so miss the one that should be fed."*[150]

Charity was Whitman's version of church. He was spiritual but not religious, yet he gave generously to all those in need, perhaps because he had struggled financially for much of his life. Doyle recalled, "Money was a thing he didn't think of as other people thought of it. It came and went, that was all there was to it."[151] At Whitman's core was a universalist faith that all people were sacred, as Pete explained. "He never went to church—didn't like form, ceremonies—didn't seem to favor preachers at all. I asked him about the hereafter. 'There must be something,' he said—'there can't be a locomotive unless there is somebody to run it.' I have heard him say that if a person was a right kind of person—and I guess he thought all persons right kind of persons—he couldn't be destroyed in the next world or this."[152]

Whitman was the very opposite of misanthropic, seeing the good in almost everyone. He remained an optimist and rarely ever got angry. That said, Pete recalled a very specific altercation with a horsecar passenger that nearly turned violent.

> *Walt's mood was very even, but I saw him mad as a March hare one night. He was on the hind end of my car, near him stood an old fellow (a carpet-bag senator—I don't know his name)—near-sighted, wore glasses, peevish, lantern-jawed, dyspeptic. They rubbed against each other. The first thing I knew there was a rumpus, the old man cussed*

The Long Bridge (now the Fourteenth Street Bridge) spanned the Potomac River between Washington, D.C., and Virginia. Walt and Pete often crossed there on their walks. *Library of Congress.*

Walt—said, "Get out of the way, you—" and Walt only answered, "Damn you!" The old man had a loaded stick with him—he raised it—would have struck Walt and perhaps killed him but I came between them just in time. I cried: "Get in the car, Walt!" (they were both in the street by this time) and I was glad to see the affair ended that way. No explanations were made. All effects of it vanished at once from Walt's face and manner. [153]

It is clear from the vast correspondence that flowed from Whitman's pen that he was close to his family. He loved his brothers and his sisters, and especially his mother, Louisa. One wonders what they thought of his being gay in an era before such words were spoken, but they surely knew Walt had same-sex attractions. Was it something they simply didn't talk about or used coded language for (like saying Walt was a "confirmed bachelor")? Peter Doyle confirmed, in so many words, Walt's sexual orientation.

I never knew a case of Walt's being bothered up by a woman. In fact, he had nothing special to do with any woman except Mrs. [Nelly] *O'Connor and Mrs.* [Ursula] *Burroughs. His disposition was different. Woman in that sense never came into his head... Towards women generally Walt had a good way—he very easily attracted them. But he did that with men, too. And it was an irresistible attraction. I've had many tell me—men and women. He had an easy, gentle way—the same for all, no matter who they were or what their sex.*[154]

Whitman traveled to Brooklyn in 1868 for a six-week family visit. Walt and Pete wrote to each other frequently. In fact, it was the beginning of two decades of correspondence between the men. In that first letter, Walt wrote, "I find it first rate to think of you, Pete, and to know that you are there all right and that I shall return and we will be together again."[155] Walt used a wide variety of salutations to address Pete in his letters, all revolving around a paternal theme: Dear Boy, Dear Boy Pete, my darling boy. Walt often referred to himself as Pete's loving comrade and father.

Walt wrote to Pete from Providence, Rhode Island, that he had met many flirtatious women at a party, adding, "I also made love to the woman, and flatter myself that I created at least one impression—wretch and gay deceiver that I am."[156] Whether he actually had sex with this woman is doubtful; it is more likely he was simply teasing Pete.

In 1869, Pete came down with an embarrassing rash on his face, which some historians have suggested was syphilis. Walt took him to a friend, Dr. Charles Bowen, who diagnosed it as "barber's itch" and treated it. It took a while to heal, during which time Pete suggested that life wasn't worth living with this condition, a suggestion that Walt took to mean suicide. Walt was upset and wrote an unusual fire-and-brimstone letter (unusual in that Walt wasn't religious): "Dear Pete, dear son, my darling boy, my young and loving brother, don't let the devil put such thoughts in your mind again—wickedness unspeakable—death and disgrace here, and hell's agonies hereafter." In fact, Pete was just being dramatic, not suicidal.[157]

That summer, in 1869, Walt was not feeling well. His health was already on the decline, despite his strong constitution, and he blamed it on the "hospital malaria" from the war. Most likely his hypertension was getting worse, exasperated by his being overweight.[158] The following summer on vacation, he wrote to Pete that he had gained several pounds, causing one person to announce, "Why Walt, you are fatter and saucier than ever."[159]

Walt's mother, Louisa, probably understood that Walt was in love with Pete. After cutting his thumb and needing a break from work, Walt took Pete to New York for a week in May 1870. They stayed in Jersey City, perhaps for privacy, given that on every other visit Walt stayed at his mother's in Brooklyn. They toured Manhattan during the day and then dined with Louisa every night. "Mrs. Whitman was a lovely woman," Pete remembered. He also observed that Walt's fondness for free rides on the omnibus hadn't ebbed. "All the omnibus drivers knew him. We always climbed up to the top of the busses, our heels hanging over."[160]

The two men did experience tempestuous moments in their relationship. In July 1870—shortly after their trip to New York—Walt expressed great exasperation with Pete in his notebook. He wrote several coded entries (16.4 refers to the letters in the alphabet, thus P and D, or Peter Doyle, and he also referred to him as "her"—either for posterity's sake or because he was concerned that Pete might read his diary). "Always preserve a kind spirits & demeanor to 16. BUT PURSUE HER NO MORE." On July 15, he wrote:

TO GIVE UP ABSOLUTELY & for good from the present hour this *FEVERISH, FLUCTUATING,* useless *UNDIGNIFIED PURSUIT OF 16.4*—too long, (much too long) *persevered in,—so humiliating,*—It must come at last & *had better come now*—(It cannot possibly be a success) *LET THERE FROM THIS HOUR BE NO FALTERING, NO GETTING* at all henceforth, *(NOT ONCE, UNDER* any circumstances)—avoid seeing her, or meeting her, or any talk or explanations—or *ANY MEETING WHATEVER, FROM THIS HOUR FORTH, FOR LIFE*[161]

Walt didn't give Pete up. The couple somehow made up. In fact, two weeks later, he wrote to Pete from his mother's home in Brooklyn: "Pete, there was something in that hour from 10 to 11 oclock (parting though it was) that has left me pleasure & comfort for good—I never dreamed that you made so much of having me with you, nor that you could feel so downcast at losing me. I foolishly thought it was all on the other side. But all I will say further on the subject is, I now see clearly, that was all wrong."[162]

Pete often complained about his job and his employers. Walt took him to task, saucily concluding an 1870 letter, "Only a good smacking kiss and many of them—and taking in return many, many, many, from my dear son—good loving ones too—which will do more credit to his lips than growling and complaining at his father."[163] Even as their romance faded after Walt's 1873 stroke, Pete and Walt maintained a lifelong friendship.

Chapter 8

O CAPTAIN! MY CAPTAIN!

B y 1865, the Confederacy was close to collapse. Atlanta had fallen the previous September. Sherman was marching almost unopposed through the Carolinas, wreaking devastation through the Southern heartland. Grant had a stranglehold on Lee's army at Petersburg and, one by one, was cutting off its supply lines. The Confederacy could no longer feed its dwindling armies or its thousands of Union prisoners. Whitman noted the large number of Rebel deserters who had given up on the "Secession army," as he called it. Wave after wave was brought through Washington that spring. They took the oath of allegiance to the United States and then were shipped off to points north and west.[164]

Most importantly, Abraham Lincoln had been reelected in November 1864 to see through the brutal Civil War and to reunite the nation. The North was on the verge of winning, and slavery's days were numbered.

That spring, the evening star had shone especially bright in the sky at dusk. "The western star, Venus, in the earlier hours of evening, has never been so large, so clear; it seems as if it told something, as if it held rapport indulgent with humanity, with us Americans," Whitman observed. "The star was wonderful, the moon like a young mother." But did it portend rebirth or twilight?[165]

Lincoln's second inauguration was held on Saturday, March 4, 1865. Walt rose early to visit the House of Representatives, which held an all-night session to finish its business in time for the new Congress to be sworn in. The day dawned gloomy and rainy, but crowds still gathered along Pennsylvania Avenue to witness the presidential procession.

Whitman walked down to the Avenue, whose condition he described as "Mud, (and such mud!)." From there, he saw the president depart for the Capitol at noon and return three hours later. Lincoln was not part of the parade: he rode in a carriage, accompanied only by his son Tad and without the usual military escort, as he had spent the morning signing newly passed bills. Walt wrote in the *New York Times,* "I never see that man without feeling that he is one to become personally attach'd to, for his combination of purest, heartiest tenderness, and native Western even rudest forms of manliness."[166]

Thousands of people assembled on the Capitol grounds to hear the president speak. Whitman might have been in the crowd, or he might have skipped the inauguration speech. He added a single sentence to his *Times* article: "As the President came out on the capitol portico, a curious little white cloud, the only one in that part of the sky, appeared like a hovering bird, right over him." Lincoln's Second Inaugural Address set the stage for Reconstruction with the famous words "with malice towards none; with charity for all." The president and the country knew that the war was almost over. In fact, it would be in just six weeks.[167]

Abraham Lincoln delivers his second inaugural address on March 4, 1865. *Library of Congress.*

Among the onlookers at the Capitol was a famous actor, John Wilkes Booth, who detested Lincoln and the abolitionist cause. More than four years earlier, Booth had disguised himself as a militiaman so he could witness John Brown's hanging.

That night, Walt ventured to the White House, where a huge crowd gathered to congratulate the president. "I saw Mr. Lincoln, drest all in black, with white kid gloves, and a claw-hammer coat, receiving, as in duty bound, shaking hands, looking very disconsolate, and as if he would give anything to be somewhere else."[168] Whitman never ventured over to shake the president's hand. It was the last time he would ever see Lincoln.

Two days later, Lincoln's inaugural ball was held at the Patent Office, the building where Whitman worked. A ticket to the ball cost ten dollars and admitted a man and two women. The entire top floor was dedicated to the ball. Attendees ascended the stairs in their ballroom finest—gowns, kid gloves, opera capes—and entered the Great Hall. They promenaded through the large east gallery, past the nine-foot cases filled with patent models and then on to the north gallery, which was set up for dancing. The doors were closed to the west hall, which was set up for a late-night buffet supper. Today, only the east hall remains architecturally identical to Whitman's day, though patent cases and models are no longer on display.

Whitman wrote about the inauguration ball for the *New York Times*, an article that became a key source for *Memoranda*. Earlier in the day, he climbed the stairs from his office to see a space that he had known as a hospital from his many visits. The colorful bunting and caterers setting up tables for the grand dinner jogged his memory to a time when the halls were used as a hospital.

I have this moment been up to look at the gorgeously arrayed ball and supper-rooms, for the Inauguration Dance aforesaid, (which begins in a few hours;) and I could not help thinking of the scene those rooms, where the music will sound and the dancers' feet presently tread—what a different scene they presented to my view a while since, filled with a crowded mass of the worst wounded of the war, brought in from Second Bull Run, Antietam and Fredericksburgh. To-night, beautiful women, perfumes, the violins' sweetness, the polka and the waltz; but then, the amputation, the blue face, the groan, the glassy eye of the dying, the clotted rag, the odor of old wounds and blood, and many a mother's son amid strangers, passing away untended there, (for the crowd of the badly hurt was great, and much for nurse to do, and much for surgeon.) Think not of such grim things, gloved ladies, as you bow to your partners, and the figures of the dance this night are loudly

called, or you may drop on the floor that has known what this one knew,
but two short winters since.[169]

Whitman was not one to spend on such extravagances, and so he skipped the ball. Dancing commenced at 10:00 p.m. President Lincoln and his wife, Mary, soon arrived. Shortly before midnight, the Lincolns were seated in the supper room, where a 250-foot table had been laid with the greatest delicacies. The doors were then opened for the attendees to take of the buffet. More than four thousand guests had bought tickets for the ball, far more than could fit in the west gallery. What followed was not one of Washington's finer moments in its social history, as the *Evening Star* reported:

> *The onset of the crowd upon the tables was frightful, and nothing but the immense reserves of eatables laid in by the thoughtful supper committee would have supplied the demand, or rather the waste. Numbers...who, with more audacity than good taste, could be seen snatching whole pates, chickens, legs of veal, halves of turkies [sic], ornamental pyramids, &c, from the tables, and bearing them aloft over the heads of the shuddering crowd, (ladies especially, with greasy ruin to their dresses impending) carry them off in triumph for private delectation. The floor of the supper room was soon sticky, pasty and oily with wasted confections, mashed cake and debris of fowl and meat.*

"Finally everybody was satisfied, even those who felt bound to 'eat their ten dollars' worth,' and the ball room again filled up, and the dance and the promenade was resumed," the eyewitness concluded, noting that people had left their plates scattered around the floor for others to step on. The Lincolns remained until 1:00 a.m. The party continued for another three hours.[170]

Soon after the inauguration, Whitman took a four-week leave home to Brooklyn to see his brother George, newly freed from a Confederate prison. Whitman needed the time off to finalize his manuscript for *Drum-Taps*. Events quickly outpaced its publication.

Confederate general Robert E. Lee surrendered at Appomattox on April 9, and the other large Confederate army in North Carolina surrendered two weeks later. The war was over. The Union armies decamped to Washington to receive their final pay and be mustered out. The city was crowded with Union soldiers eager to return home. The feeling was one of euphoria in the nation's capital.

The Great Hall of the Patent Office hosted Lincoln's second inaugural ball on March 6, 1865. *Library of Congress.*

LINCOLN'S ASSASSINATION

On April 14, 1865, the *Evening Star* noted that General Grant would accompany President Lincoln to Ford's Theatre that evening to see the play *Our American Cousin.*[171] Grant had just arrived in Washington from Lee's surrender at Appomattox, but his wife, Julia, loathed Mary Lincoln and declined the invitation. Lincoln found another couple to join them: Major Henry Rathbone and Clara Harris. Ford's Theatre was just two blocks from where Whitman worked in the Patent Office.

Walt was in Brooklyn, so his friend Peter Doyle ventured out that evening alone. He bought a ticket for the performance and walked upstairs to his seat. "I heard that the President and his wife would be present and made up my mind to go," Doyle explained. "There was a great crowd in the building. I got into the second gallery. There was nothing extraordinary in the performance. I saw everything on the stage and was in a good position to see the President's box."

Actor John Wilkes Booth was determined to kill President Lincoln that evening, though he had long fostered other ideas. He had wanted to kidnap Mr. Lincoln and hold him hostage in Richmond to force the North to sue for peace. With the conclusion of the war, however, kidnapping him became pointless. Enraged by Lincoln's talk of black suffrage, Booth decided to

Ford's Theatre was the site of the Lincoln assassination. *Library of Congress.*

assassinate him while his fellow conspirators murdered leading abolitionists in the cabinet—Vice President Andrew Johnson and Secretary of State William Seward—all on the same night.

Booth knew the theater well, as well as the play. He quietly entered the president's box and aimed his derringer at the back of Lincoln's head. He waited for the audience to laugh at a particular joke and then pulled the trigger. "I heard the pistol shot," Doyle said. "I had no idea what it was, what it meant—it was sort of muffled. I really knew nothing of what had occurred until Mrs. Lincoln leaned out of the box and cried, 'The President is shot!' I needn't tell you what I felt then, or saw. It is all put down in Walt's piece—that piece is exactly right."

Booth stabbed Major Rathbone with a knife and then jumped down to the stage below. "I saw Booth on the cushion of the box, saw him jump over, saw him catch his foot, which turned, saw him fall on the stage. He got up on his feet, cried out something which I could not hear for the hub-bub"—it was "*Sic semper tyrannis!*"—"and disappeared. I suppose I lingered almost the last person. A soldier came into the gallery, saw me still there, called to me:

John Wilkes Booth assassinated President Abraham Lincoln at Ford's Theatre on April 14, 1865. *Library of Congress.*

'Get out of here! we're going to burn this damned building down!' I said: 'If that is so I'll get out!'"[172] Ford's Theatre was not torn down but survives as a live performance stage and a museum to Lincoln's assassination.

Booth broke his ankle falling to the stage, but he managed to escape the theater and fled over the Navy Yard Bridge to Maryland. Lincoln was mortally injured, but the other two planned assassinations failed. The evening's most violent confrontation took place at Seward's mansion. Assassin Lewis Powell entered the Seward home and violently assaulted Seward's sons Fred and Gus, as well as a nurse, George Robinson, before turning his knife on the secretary of state. However, he succeeded only in gruesomely slicing Seward's face and then stabbed a State Department clerk as he fled. A third assassin, George Atzerodt, was to kill Vice President Andrew Johnson at the Kirkwood House hotel but decided not to.

Lincoln's unconscious body was carried across the street from Ford's Theatre to William Petersen's boardinghouse, and there he died the following day at 7:22 a.m. The nation was stunned. The man who had led the United States through a grueling Civil War was gone. Secretary of War Edwin Stanton immediately began the prosecution of the assassins, and the U.S. government offered a $10,000 reward for their capture, including that of John Wilkes Booth.[173]

With the telegraph lines, news traveled quickly. Whitman learned of Lincoln's death that morning while at his mother's house in Brooklyn. He recalled, "Mother prepared breakfast—and other meals afterwards—as usual, but not a mouthful was eaten all day by either of us. We each drank half a cup of coffee; that was all." They spent the morning reading the newspapers in silence.[174]

Later that morning, Walt ventured out of the house, over the Brooklyn ferry to Manhattan. He walked his old haunts on Broadway. All commerce had stopped. "All Broadway is black with mourning—the façades of the houses are festooned with black," he wrote in a notebook. "Towards noon the sky darkened & it began to rain. Drip, drip, & heavy moist black weather—the stores are all closed—the rain sent the women from the street & black clothed men only remain."[175]

Walt collected his thoughts about Lincoln. "He leaves, in my opinion, the greatest, best, most characteristic, artistic, moral personality," he wrote in his notebook the next day. Whitman had come to love the president, above all for his commitment to the Union, a quality he saw as a virtue. "He was assassinated—but the Union is not assassinated," he wrote. "Death does its work, obliterates a hundred, a thousand—President, general, captain, private—but the Nation is immortal."[176] Lincoln's death spawned the national unity that Whitman had long hoped for. Even the recently defeated South was appalled at the assassination.

John Wilkes Booth evaded his pursuers for twelve days, crossing the Potomac River at night into Virginia. Union troops finally cornered him in a barn near Port Royal. He was shot and killed there, though his fellow conspirator, David Herold, surrendered.

THE LINCOLN ELEGIES

Lincoln's public funeral in Washington was held on April 19, five days after the assassination. The president's remains were then taken by railroad on a long, circuitous route to eleven cities before reaching their final destination in Springfield, Illinois, for his burial. It was the first time that a president had ever had such a funeral train. The nation grieved, as did Whitman. The day of the Washington funeral, Walt composed the first of four poems about Lincoln, "Hush'd Be the Camps To-day." The short poem began:

Hush'd be the camps to-day,
And soldiers let us drape our war-worn weapons,
And each with musing soul to retire to celebrate,
Our dear commander's death.

Whitman suspended the publication of *Drum-Taps*. Events had overtaken the book—his return to Washington to assume a federal job, the end of the Civil War and, above all, President Lincoln's assassination. He understood that the volume was instantly out of date and began adding poems that dealt with the nation's grief over the loss of Lincoln. He was already working on a sequel that would include two of his best-known poems, "O Captain! My

Lincoln's funeral procession on Pennsylvania Avenue on April 19, 1865. *Library of Congress.*

119

Captain!" and "When Lilacs Last in the Dooryard Bloom'd," the latter of which is considered Whitman's last great poem.[177]

"O Captain! My Captain!" was Whitman's most famous and popular poem, one that he would read to the public at the end of his famous Lincoln lecture. "O Captain!" is an allegorical poem about Lincoln bringing his ship (the United States) safely into harbor and then dying. It even included a dream that Lincoln supposedly experienced.

> *O Captain! my Captain! our fearful trip is done,*
> *The ship has weather'd every rack, the prize we sought is won,*
> *The port is near, the bells I hear, the people all exulting,*
> *While follow eyes the steady keel, the vessel grim and daring;*
> *But O heart! heart! heart!*
> *O the bleeding drops of red,*
> *Where on the deck my Captain lies,*
> *Fallen cold and dead.*

Most literary critics agree it is not one of Whitman's finer poems, but it certainly is his most famous. It has been damned with faint praise that it is conventional and that it has a poetic meter and rhyme. "O Captain!" is very un-Whitmanesque. (The opening line may have originated from Herman Melville's *Moby-Dick*, published in 1851, where first mate Starbuck tried to reason with the insane captain Ahab to give up the hunt for the white whale: "Oh, my Captain! my Captain! noble soul! grand old heart, after all! why should any one give chase to that hated fish!") Whitman later remarked, "Damn My Captain...I'm almost sorry I ever wrote the poem."[178]

According to Whitman's friend John Burroughs, Whitman began composing his greatest Lincoln elegy, "When Lilacs Last in the Dooryard Bloom'd," within several weeks of Lincoln's death.[179] It is one of Walt's most beautiful poems, written in free verse and filled with mystical visions and powerful, tragic imagery that he experienced that spring in Washington. A trinity of objects derived from nature replaced the Christian Holy Trinity: the blooming lilac; the shy, warbling thrush; and the bright star that appeared at twilight and then fell below the horizon. Lilacs bloomed in April and May—they were everywhere in Washington, fragrant with lavender blossoms. Whitman learned about the thrush from John Burroughs, who was an expert ornithologist. (The thrush was a shy bird that lives in the shadows; Burroughs probably pointed out the bird to Walt during their hikes.) The star was the planet Venus, which had shone strongly at dusk.

In "When Lilacs Last in the Dooryard Bloom'd," Whitman captured the sense of national mourning as Lincoln's funeral train passed through the cities of the North and thousands of people turned out to pay their respects for the fallen president:

Coffin that passes through lanes and streets,
Through day and night with the great cloud darkening the land,
With the pomp of the inloop'd flags with the cities draped in black,
With the show of the States themselves as of crape-veil'd women standing,
With processions long and winding and the flambeaus of the night,
With the countless torches lit, with the silent sea of faces with unbarred heads,
With the waiting depot, the arriving coffin, and the sombre faces,
With dirges through the night, with the thousand voices rising strong and solemn,
With all the mournful voices of the dirges pour'd around the coffin,
The dim-lit churches and the shuddering organs—where amid these you journey,
With the tolling tolling bells' perpetual clang,
Here, coffin that slowly passes,
I give you my sprig of lilac.

Venus shone bright in the twilight sky and then disappeared over the horizon into the netherworld. The star stood for Lincoln, once bright and shimmering but now gone forever:

O western orb sailing the heaven,
Now I know what you must have meant as a month since I walk'd,
As I walk'd in silence the transparent shadowy night,
As I saw you had something to tell as you bent to me night after night,
As you droop'd from the sky low down as if to by my side, (while the other
*   stars all look'd on,)*
As we wander'd together the solemn night, (for something I know not what
*   kept me from sleep,)*
As the night advanced, and I saw on the rim of the west how full you were
*   of woe,*
As I stood on the rising ground in the breeze in the cool transparent night,
As I watch'd where you pass'd and was lost in the netherward black of
*   the night,*
As my soul in its trouble dissatisfied sank, as where you sad orb,
Concluded, dropt in the night, and was gone.

Joined by two companions—the knowledge of death and the thought of death—the narrator fled down a dim path to shores of a swamp, "to the solemn shadowy cedars and ghostly pines so still." The waters bordered the underworld, like the River Styx that separated the living world from Hades in Greek mythology. And there the hermit thrush sang a lovely paean to death. Whitman then experienced a vision of the war, of the armies and their battle flags, but all was silent. And he felt both the living and the dead in his presence:

I saw battle-corpses, myriads of them,
And the white skeletons of young men, I saw them,
I saw the debris and debris of all the slain soldiers of the war,
But I saw they were not as was thought,
They themselves were fully at rest, they suffer'd not,
The living remain'd and suffer'd, the mother suffer'd,
And the wife and the child and the musing comrade suffer'd,
And the armies that remain'd suffer'd.

The living suffer, but the dead do not. And thus, for both Lincoln and the soldiers who had fought a grueling Civil War to reunite the country and to end slavery, the dead are at rest, but the living carry the burden of grief for their lost love ones. Whitman concluded the elegy:

Comrades mine and I in the midst, and their memory ever to keep, for the
dead I loved so well,
For the sweetest, wisest soul of all my days and lands—and this for his
dear sake,
Lilac and star and bird twined with the chant of my soul,
There in the fragrant pines and the cedars dusk and dim.

"Lilacs" is a remarkable poem for its use of historical subtext. It never mentions Lincoln or even his assassination, nor does it include Christian imagery or Lincoln's martyrdom. (The president was murdered on Good Friday, and newly freed slaves considered him a modern-day Moses.) There is no promise of an afterlife, only an end of suffering through death. Whitman bypassed many of the cultural references of his day that might be expected in an elegy. Instead, he composed a poem that was almost Buddhist in its sentiment. And Walt broadened "Lilacs" beyond just the fallen president to include everyone who had lived through the Civil War, both living and dead.

Whitman would later compose an essay and a lecture of the Lincoln assassination, largely based on Peter Doyle's account. And he would write one final poem about the president. In 1871, Whitman wrote a short, thirty-word epitaph that was his fourth poem about Lincoln:

This dust was once the man
Gentle, plain, just resolute, under whose cautious hand,
Against the foulest crime in history known in any land or age,
Was saved the Union of these States.

Through these four poems—but, above all, through "Lilacs"—Whitman delivered Lincoln's greatest elegies. But it's a curious fact: Whitman may or may not have attended Lincoln's inauguration speech, and he certainly did not attend the inauguration ball. In fact, he missed Lincoln's assassination and funeral as well. He never even got to shake hands or speak with the man he adored. But he immortalized Lincoln with his poetry.

Chapter 9

DRUM-TAPS

Patience and patronage were required to obtain federal employment in the nineteenth century. Every job, in essence, was a political appointment. There were no civil service exams for the country's first century, though that would change after President James Garfield's assassination by a failed patronage seeker.

Whitman had applied for federal work soon after he arrived in Washington in 1863, but his appeal on literary grounds fell on deaf ears. If anything, the publication of *Leaves of Grass* made him controversial, and no one was willing to sponsor him for employment. But after he had spent several years volunteering at hospitals, people changed their minds.

Walt was in Brooklyn on his seven-month hiatus from Washington when he received a letter from his friend William O'Connor, dated December 30, 1864, offering an opening as a federal clerk. A senior federal executive, J. Hubley Ashton, admired Whitman's poetry and put in a word with Secretary of the Interior William Otto to get Walt a job. Walt needed to write Otto a letter requesting employment. "Now, dear Walt, do this without delay," O'Connor instructed. "The object of your writing the letter is to get a specimen of your hand. Pick out, then, a good pen and write as fairly as you can a letter formally applying for a clerkship. Then enclose a *copy* of this letter to Ashton, so that he can follow it in to the Secretary."[180]

Whitman did as he was told and soon had a job offer in the Department of the Interior, working in the Bureau of Indian Affairs. When he responded to O'Connor on January 6, 1865, Walt noted that he hoped to publish

Drum-Taps that winter, a book that he thought superior to *Leaves of Grass*. He described his literary hopes:

> *But I am perhaps mainly satisfied with* Drum-Taps *because it delivers my ambition of the task that has haunted me, namely, to express in a poem (& in the way I like, which is not at all by directly stating it) the pending action of this* Time & Land we swim in, *with all their large conflicting fluctuations of despair & hope, the shiftings, masses, & the whirl & deafening din, (yet over all, as by invisible hand, a definite purport & idea)—with the unprecedented anguish of wounded & suffering, the beautiful young men, in wholesome death & agony, everything sometimes as if in blood color, & dripping blood.*[181]

Whitman returned to Washington and started work as a federal employee on January 24—coincidentally the same day that a massive fire burned the top floor of the Smithsonian Castle. His career began in the Patent Office building as a first-class clerk, earning $1,200 per year. One week into the new job, Whitman wrote to his brother Jeff describing the work:

> *It is easy enough—I take things very easy—the rule is to come at 9 and go at 4—but I don't come at 9, and only stay till 4 when I want, as at present to finish a letter for the mail—I am treated with great courtesy, as an evidence of which I have to inform you that since I began this letter, I have been sent for by the cashier to receive my PAY for the arduous & invaluable service I have already rendered to the government.*[182]

During the five months that Walt worked in the Bureau of Indian Affairs, he got to meet many Indian chiefs who came to Washington to negotiate treaties and reservations. (Over the years, a number of Indian delegation members died in the city and are buried in Congressional Cemetery.) Whitman marveled at the Indians that he met. "Every head and face is impressive, even artistic," he later wrote with admiration in *November Boughs*. They wore their finest ceremonial attire, carrying tomahawks and rich ornaments and headdresses, and most were wrapped in scarlet blankets. One even wore an empty buffalo skull on his head. Walt continued: "Their feathers, paint—even the empty buffalo skull—did not, to say the least, seem any more ludicrous to me [than] many of the fashions I have seen in civilized society. I would not apply the word savage (at any rate, in the usual sense) as a leading word in the description of those great aboriginal specimens, of whom I certainly saw many of the best."[183]

Even as Whitman settled into federal employment, his brother George languished in a Confederate prison. Walt and Jeff went to work campaigning for their brother's release.

GEORGE WHITMAN: FREE AT LAST

On September 30, 1864, Whitman's brother George and most of his regiment were captured near Petersburg, Virginia. George was first taken to Libby Prison in Richmond, and then he and other officers were transferred to a tobacco warehouse in Danville, which was converted into a jail for Union officers. There he fell ill in the overcrowded, malnourished conditions. For several weeks the Whitman family fretted that George might be dead, but letters from a Confederate prison arrived. George mailed several letters home while a prisoner-of-war to let his family know that he was alive, including on October 2 and October 23.[184] Jeff and Walt forwarded a care package of food, but it didn't reach George for months. Walt wrote an angry op-ed in the *New York Times* deploring the situation and recounting the Fifty-first New York's gallant service.[185]

In 1863, the Union began arming former slaves into regiments to fight against the South. Whenever a black soldier was taken prisoner, the Confederates assumed he was an escaped slave and refused to exchange him for a white soldier. Rather than exchange just white prisoners, the U.S. government put a halt to all prisoner exchanges until the Confederacy agreed to exchange black soldiers as well. George Whitman was caught in this impasse.

On December 26, George's army trunk arrived in Brooklyn. The family spent the day unpacking it, finding uniforms, letters and photos and a small campaign diary. It dampened their spirits: they had not heard from George since October, and they feared that he might be starving in prison.[186] The next day, Walt lashed out at the U.S. government's policy of halting the prisoner exchanges. He published simultaneous opinion pieces in the *Brooklyn Daily Eagle* and the *New York Times*. With clear exasperation, Walt asked: "Whose fault is it at bottom that our men have not been exchanged?" He blamed the generals and Secretary of War Edwin Stanton for allowing tens of thousands of soldiers to starve to death in prisoner-of-war camps, as the Confederacy had no capacity to feed them.[187]

Jeff came up with a politically ingenious way to push for George's exchange. On January 31, 1865, he wrote to Walt, asking him to send a letter to their mutual friend John Swinton, editor of the *New York Times*. "Now I am positive that a letter could be got from Swinton to [General] Grant signed as Editor of the *Times* asking that a speical [*sic*] exchange might be made in George's case," he reasoned.[188] Walt wrote to Swinton. The prison exchanges resumed in February when the Confederacy agreed to exchange black soldiers, but this was probably coincidental. It is difficult to assess how effective the Whitman brothers' campaign was.

While a stream of Union soldiers was released from Confederate prisons, the Whitmans waited nervously all month for George to appear. He wasn't in the first waves. Finally, George was exchanged on February 22 after five months as a prisoner of war. He wrote his mother two days later from Annapolis, Maryland, to let her know that he was coming home and that he had gotten the box of food in Richmond that Jeff and Walt had sent months earlier.[189]

George was one of the more fortunate ones of his regiment. Of the 325 soldiers and 8 officers captured, only 90 would return. The others died in Confederate prisons.[190] When George was released, he earned a thirty-day pass home starting on March 5 (the day after the Lincoln inauguration), though he stayed longer because his health was still recovering. Walt joined the family in Brooklyn within days, having asked for a leave of absence from work to see his brother and to work on *Drum-Taps*.

George Whitman returned to active duty around April 24. After having fought in many of the major battles of the Civil War, he missed the climactic ending: the breaking of the siege of Petersburg and Lee's surrender at Appomattox Court House. His days in combat were over. George's regiment was stationed at Camp Augur near Alexandria, Virginia. It was a convenient place for Walt to visit until George had court-martial duty that kept him busy. On July 14, George wrote to his brother, "Walt come over and see us, the stage leaves Willards [Hotel] twice every day, and brings you right to camp, so jump in and come over."[191] During George's sojourn in Alexandria, Walt ventured over the Potomac to dine with him at least twice.[192]

George briefly served as the commander of the Prince Street Military Prison (it still stands at 200 South Fairfax Street). "I have about 300 Prisoners (mostly thieves, Bounty jumpers and Deserters) to look after," he explained in a letter to his mother. "There is [*sic*] about 20 Rebel Officers here (Paroled Prisoners) but they are used very different from what we were, when we were in Rebeldom."[193]

THE GRAND REVIEW

With the end of the war, the armies began returning home, and the regiments mustered out. But first there were victory parades through the nation's capital—days and days of parades to celebrate the proud soldiers who had won the war. Whitman noted that there were so many soldiers in the capital that "you see them swarming like bees everywhere."[194]

The Army of the Potomac assembled east of the Capitol and then paraded down Pennsylvania Avenue on May 23. General Sherman's army, freshly returned from the Carolinas, paraded through the city the next day. Altogether some 200,000 Union soldiers passed in review before President Andrew Johnson, like a triumphal march of the conquering armies through ancient Rome. Whitman witnessed the spectacle—and perhaps Peter Doyle joined him. The Grand Review followed the route of the horsecar line, meaning that service was interrupted during the parades. Walt wrote:

> *For two days now the broad spaces of Pennsylvania Avenue along to Treasury Hill, and so by detour around the President's House, (and so up to Georgetown, and across the Aqueduct bridge,) have been alive with a magnificent sight, the returning Armies. In their wide ranks stretching clear across the Avenue, I watch them march or ride along, at a brisk pace, through two whole days—Infantry, Cavalry, Artillery—some 200,000 men. Some days afterwards one or two other Corps; and then, still afterwards, a good part of Sherman's immense Army, brought up from Charleston, Savannah, &c.*[195]

The weather had already turned hot, and a number of men suffered sunstroke or heat exhaustion during the Grand Review. "Some of these shows cost the lives of scores of men," Walt noted ruefully.[196]

George and his regiment were mustered out on July 25. Two days later, they marched from Alexandria to the B&O Railroad station in Washington, where a train would take them home to New York. Walt went with the regiment to the train station to say goodbye. He wrote in a notebook, "The long train, carrying other regiments also, as it bent round a curve, some twenty cars, the roofs also covered with men, clustering on like bees, was quite a sight."[197] George returned to civilian life, eventually becoming a successful pipe inspector in Camden, New Jersey.

Walt was very proud of his brother's military service, and he wrote several admiring op-eds about George's accomplishments for the *Brooklyn*

Matthew Brady photographed Sherman's army as it marched up Pennsylvania Avenue in the Grand Review on May 24, 1865. The army followed the horsecar route on which Peter Doyle worked. *Library of Congress*

Daily Union (March 16 and August 5, 1865). George had enlisted as a private and ended the war as a lieutenant colonel. In recalling his brother's distinguished service—including seeing combat at Second Bull Run, Antietam, Fredericksburg, Vicksburg, the Wilderness, Spotsylvania, Cold Harbor and the siege at Petersburg and then being taken prisoner— Whitman understood the deep patriotism that arose from countless families such as his.

I strengthen and comfort myself much with the certainty for just such Regiments, (hundreds, thousands of them) is inexhaustible in the United

An April 1864 image of the officers' quarters at Harewood Hospital. In the distance is the newly completed Capitol dome. Harewood was the last Civil War hospital in Washington to close in April 1866. *Library of Congress.*

States, and that there isn't a County nor a Township in The Republic—nor a street in any City—but could turn out, and, on occasion, would *turn out, lots of just such* Typical Soldiers, *whenever wanted.*[198]

Thousands of emaciated Union prisoners of war were freed from Confederate camps, a horrific mass of men who had suffered starvation and deprivation. Nearly half a million men were disabled from wounds during the war, in addition to the more than 600,000 who were killed. "The war is over, but the hospitals are fuller than ever," Whitman wrote.[199] Wounds took time to heal. Walt's federal job left him with free time to continue his hospital visits. The hospitals themselves began consolidating and closing as the patients returned home. By November 1865, only Harewood Hospital was still open. Harewood was once a farm near the Soldiers' Home owned by banker William Wilson Corcoran, who had sympathized with the Confederacy and spent the war in Europe. Even that closed its gates in April 1866, a full year after the war ended.

THE LINCOLN CONSPIRACY TRIAL

On May 1, 1865, eight people were brought before a military tribunal in the Washington Arsenal and charged with conspiring to kill President Lincoln. The tribunal convicted all of them on July 6. It ordered four of them (George Atzerodt, David Herold, Lewis Powell and Mary Surratt) to be hanged the next day. There is nothing in the record to indicate if Whitman attended any of the tribunal. He was working at the Bureau of Indian Affairs, and when he had free time, he was still very busy with hospital visits.

Only two hundred passes were issued to watch the conspirators' execution, including photographer Alexander Gardner, who captured the moment with his lens. Whitman likely did not witness the execution. He had seen enough death already.

However, Walt did attend the 1867 trial of John Surratt, Anna Surratt's son, who had served as a Washington-based courier for the Confederate Secret Service. Surratt was in New York when Lincoln was assassinated, and he immediately fled to Canada and then boarded ship to Europe. He was uncovered in Rome and then apprehended in Egypt. He was extradited to the United States for trial in a criminal court rather than a military tribunal, which is what had condemned Surratt's mother. Whitman wrote to Alfred Pratt: "It is very interesting to sit & hear the witnesses & the speeches of the lawyers. It has been a tedious trial, & it is hard to tell how it will end." The jury could not reach a verdict, so Surratt was set free. He was charged once again in 1868, only to be released.[200]

Photographer Alexander Gardner captured the hanging of four Lincoln conspirators on July 7, 1865. *Library of Congress.*

Washington gradually returned to its peacetime routines. The wooden barracks and hospitals were torn down. By August 1865, there were far fewer soldiers on the city's streets. "Blue coats here are getting quite scarce," Walt wrote to a friend.[201] A year later, there were virtually no soldiers to be seen. Whitman lamented the loss of the soldiers and the constant air of excitement. "Washington is rather dull—no more soldiers around like there used to be—no more patrols marching through the streets—no more great racks of hospitals—I get along well enough in this city in pleasant weather, when one can go around, but it's rough in bad weather," he wrote to another friend, Alfred Pratt.[202]

DRUM-TAPS

As the hospitals emptied, Whitman was finally able to return to his book of poetry about the Civil War. He published *Sequel to Drum-Taps*, which included the Lincoln elegy "Lilacs," in October 1865. He called the volume "Walt Whitman's second wind."[203] Walt gave Peter Doyle the original manuscript, but during a move, it was somehow lost or stolen. "At the time I did not appreciate it as I should now," Pete later remarked.[204]

Drum-Taps sealed Whitman's reputation as America's Civil War poet. History has accorded it as a great book of poetry, yet its immediate reception was mixed. Henry James, a budding, brilliant novelist, thought ill of Whitman's poetry. After reading *Drum-Taps*, he wrote scathingly in *The Nation*: "His volume is an offense against art." James took offense at Whitman's prosaic style of composing: "Prose, in order to be good poetry, must first be good prose." For blowing his own horn, James labeled him "tolerably egotistical."[205] James was still a young man and, later in life, came to regret how harshly he had written about Whitman, especially once Walt's reputation as a poet had been established. Likewise, William Dean Howells was not a fan of Whitman's new volume. He wrote a mean review of *Drum-Taps* in the *Round Table*, calling it "unspeakably inartistic."[206] This was the same man who later recalled meeting Walt at Pfaff's and was struck by his humanity.

A full year after *Drum-Taps* was published, one of Whitman's best friends, John Burroughs, reviewed it in the *Galaxy*. He called it "full of warlike passion, singularly blended with as much sadness, perhaps, as was ever printed in a like space." Burroughs spent considerable time covering the musical and natural qualities of the book's best poem, "When Lilacs Last in the Dooryard Bloom'd."[207]

In his twilight years, Walt told biographer Horace Traubel, "What the government didn't get from me in the office it got from me in the hospitals. If there is any balance in that matter I don't imagine it's on my side: not that I overvalue myself: only, the fact remains that I threw myself body and soul into that public work and came out of it without a cent and with my health shattered. But I always say, as you know: thank God I had the chance! I regret nothing!"[208]

Chapter 10
PLEASANTLY DISAPPOINTED

Before the Civil War, Whitman followed Emerson's teachings of self-reliance and individualism with the "I" at the center of his life and his poetry. After the war, he was part of the institution—a federal employee. Walt himself would eventually become a national institution in his later years.

Whitman became a full-time federal clerk in January 1865. He was not highly paid—no one in the federal civil service was—but he had a decent, lower-middle-class life. He could afford a nice room in a boardinghouse.

As did many Americans of the era, Whitman had beautiful penmanship. Walt's handwriting was crucial for his career as a federal clerk: the clerks wrote hundreds of letters each week and hand copied endless federal documents, as there were no copy machines yet and the first commercially successful typewriter wasn't invented until 1868. Most printing was done by hand. It was tedious but necessary work to keep the government running. In 2011, Professor Kenneth Price of the University of Nebraska–Lincoln uncovered some three thousand official documents in the National Archives written by Whitman.

Richard Hinton, a wounded Union soldier whom Walt had befriended in a hospital and who later became a Whitman defender, wrote in 1871 about how contemporary writers made so little money from their work. He noted that many were to be found as federal clerks, where they earned reliable paychecks while likewise having the time to write. Whitman was one of those: "He is poor; he earns little money from his literary

A signed photograph of Walt Whitman from 1863. *Library of Congress.*

productions, and yet his position is a security. His salary will support him, and his work takes little of his time and none of his thought, yet he does, perhaps, generally as much labor as the ordinary clerk."[209]

Over the years, Walt got to meet many other federal clerks. In 1888, he told Horace Traubel about his work experience, which was as true then as it is today:

I went to Washington as everybody goes there, prepared to see everything done with some furtive intention, but I was disappointed—pleasantly disappointed. I found the clerks mainly earnest, mainly honest, anxious to do the right thing—very hard working, very attentive. Why, the clerk jobs are often the worst slavery: the clerks are not overpaid, they are underpaid.[210]

Whitman's best friend, fellow author and literary champion William O'Connor championed pay raises for federal clerks. In February 1865, he took up his pen as part of a committee that examined pay increases for clerks. It addressed the high inflation of the war period that had eroded the clerks' wages and made it nigh on impossible for them to support their families. Many clerks had abandoned the federal government in favor of the private sector, where wages were far higher. O'Connor argued passionately for a pay increase.

What is the Treasury Department? It is, in one word, the banking and business house of the nation. What is the amount involved in its transactions?

Not less this year than fifteen hundred millions of dollars. Who execute and administer this gigantic business? The Secretary and Assistant Secretary? The Heads of Bureaus? The Auditors and Comptrollers? No. They do much; their functions are vast, onerous, difficult; but not being omnipotent or ubiquitous—not even having the hundred eyes of Argus, nor the hundred arms of Briareus, they can only do a part, and it is by no means the greatest part. Who, then, do the greatest part? The clerks.

O'Connor's argument, published in the report "Salaries of Clerks" in February 1865, won them a 20 percent salary increase.[211]

Even with full-time federal employment, Whitman continued taking annual leave to visit his mother in Brooklyn, during which he often worked on his next publications. His trips were usually four to eight weeks, during which he didn't get paid. But then again, money was never very important to Walt.

WHITMAN'S DISMISSAL & REHIRING

In 1865, President Andrew Johnson appointed Iowa senator James Harlan as secretary of the interior. Harlan was a former Methodist minister. In May, he issued a memoranda that the department would henceforth "be governed upon the principles of Christian civilization," as William O'Connor described it. Harlan demanded a report of subversive or immoral employees.[212]

One night after office hours, Harlan was walking around the empty desks in the Patent Office when he found a copy of the 1860 version of *Leaves of Grass* in Whitman's desk. Whitman insisted that the book was in a private drawer and that the secretary rummaged through his belongings to find it. The book was heavily marked up, as Walt was revising the text for the fourth edition, which he would publish in 1867. According to Whitman's version of the events, "He found in the book in some of these marked passages, matter so outrageous, that he had determined to discharge the author."[213]

On June 30, Walt received a one-line memo from Secretary Harlan: "The services of Walter Whitman of New York as a Clerk in the Indian Office will be dispensed with from and after this date."[214] He and about eighty other clerks were summarily dismissed without cause (among those dismissed was Clara Barton). "I found on its payrolls a considerable number of useless incumbents who were seldom at their respective desks," Harlan later explained in 1894. "Deeming it my duty to administer the business of the Department economically as well as efficiently, I endeavored, with the aid of the heads of bureaus, to weed out the needless and worthless material."[215] Either Harlan's memory had faded, or he had glossed over the unpleasantries from the controversial firing. For one, William Dole—Whitman's bureau chief—had been let go (Dole had refused to comply with the directive).

Outraged, William O'Connor sprung into action, bursting into Assistant Attorney General Hubley Ashton's office with Whitman's pink slip. Ashton got an earful from the angry

Secretary of the Interior James Harlan fired Walt Whitman on June 30, 1865, after finding a marked-up copy of *Leaves of Grass* in Whitman's desk. *Library of Congress.*

O'Connor. "I fancy that there never was before such an outpouring of impassioned eloquence in the presence of an audience of *one*," Ashton wrote.

Ashton had a cooler head than O'Connor, and he promised to appeal to Harlan. They met that afternoon. "Secretary Harlan was essentially a good and kind man, but he was capable of bitter prejudices and strong resentments, and he had, of course, great power and influence in the Government in the time," Ashton recalled. During their meeting, Harlan outright refused to rehire Whitman. According to Walt's transcript of the discussion (which he learned about secondhand), Harlan said: "It's no use Mr. Ashton—I will not have the author of that book in this Department—No, if the President of the United States should order his reinstatement, I would resign sooner than I would put him back."[216]

Ashton pointed out the considerable service that Whitman had done for the government during the war as a hospital volunteer and that Whitman was a person of considerably different character than one might assume from reading the steamier passages of *Leaves of Grass*. Harlan backed down but just a little. He promised that he would not oppose the poet from taking another government position. With this opening, Ashton then presented

A Civil War–era photograph of the Treasury Building, where Whitman worked for much of his federal career. *Library of Congress.*

a plan to his boss, Attorney General James Speed, to transfer Walt to the Attorney General's Office. Speed approved. The very next day, Walt began his new job, which was located in the Treasury Department Building.

Ashton observed that Whitman's transfer to the Attorney General's Office was a positive change in Whitman's life. The attorney general respected and liked him. "As his work was light, he was able to devote a good portion of his time to his correspondence and the revision of his writings. He had the gratification of seeing then the dawn of the day of his great fame," Ashton wrote. Indeed, it was Whitman's firing that had led in part to his great fame.[217]

Twentieth-century literary critic H.L. Mencken celebrated that Whitman was fired, as it helped propel Walt into literary stardom: "Let us remember this event and this man [Harlan]; he is too precious to die. Let us repair, once a year, to our accustomed houses of worship and there give thanks to God that one day in 1865 brought together the greatest poet America ever produced and the damndest ass."[218] Mencken was overly harsh in his treatment of Harlan: the man was no imbecile. Harlan saw that he had too many employees (Walt himself admitted he was underemployed in his January letter to his brother Jeff) and so sought to cut the roles of deadweight.

Whitman's firing was perhaps the best thing that happened to him. Unlike the other eighty clerks who simply had to find new work, Whitman was now a martyr. And unlike the other dismissed clerks, only Whitman had a literary champion in William O'Connor. O'Connor was Walt's greatest literary defender and apologist. He would brook no criticism of Whitman in print.

Outraged by Harlan's actions, O'Connor took up his pen in Walt's defense. He wrote a forty-six-page polemic, *The Good Gray Poet: A Vindication*, virulently defending Whitman and his poetry and conferring on Whitman the status of living saint for Walt's work in the hospitals. O'Connor's pamphlet was a bold move, a public criticism of a senior government official that could have cost O'Connor his job. However, by the time the pamphlet was published in January 1866, Harlan had already been reelected to the U.S. Senate.

O'Connor's pamphlet was hagiography; however, he was correct about one vital aspect. O'Connor placed Whitman in the pantheon of poets: "His place is beside Shakespeare, Aeschylus, Cervantes, Dante, Homer, Isaiah—the bards of the last ascent, the brothers of the radiant summit." Indeed, Whitman is considered one of history's greatest poets.[219]

Whitman had carefully crafted his earlier public image as "one of the roughs," but *The Good Gray Poet* altered that perception. The nickname stuck, and Whitman thereafter propagated this new myth. Many came to view Whitman as a near saint and prophet rather than just a man who was trying to drum up public attention while securing his reputation as America's foremost poet.[220]

Two years later, O'Connor published *The Carpenter*, a novella with Whitman clearly serving as the title character. "He wrote it in the attic of our house in Washington, on Capitol Hill, keeping up on tea and tobacco," John Burroughs wrote. O'Connor feverishly wrote far into the night on the story, which had at its heart the reunification of an embittered family whose two sons fought on opposing sides of the Civil War. The book further cemented Walt's reputation as a healer.[221]

WHITMAN'S FEDERAL CLERK YEARS

Whitman served as a federal clerk between 1865 and 1874, a term that ended with his disabling stroke, which forever put an end to his working career. After being fired from the Bureau of Indian Affairs, he found himself in a very comfortable situation in the Attorney General's Office. Walt had charge of expanding the library, and "the view down the river and off along Virginia hills opposite is most delightful," he wrote to John Burroughs.[222]

The work was also quite interesting. He served as a clerk in the pardon office, and he saw a parade of notable Confederates pass by his desk as they petitioned the government to reinstate their citizenship. Whitman described the job to his friend Alfred Pratt:

> *I am working now in the Attorney General's office. This is the place where the big southerners now come up to get pardoned—all the rich men & big officers of the reb army have to get special pardons, before they can buy or sell, or do any thing that will stand law—Sometimes there is a steady stream of them coming in here—old & young, men & women—some of the men are odd looking characters—I talk with them often, & find it very interesting to listen to their descriptions of things that have happened down south, & to how things are there now, &c. There are between 4 & 5000 pardons issued from this Office, but only about 200 have been signed by the President* [Andrew Johnson]—*The rest he is letting wait, till he gets good and ready.*[223]

Because of his excellent detail as a clerk, Whitman returned from his annual Brooklyn vacation in the fall of 1866 to discover that he had been promoted to third-class clerk. This came with a nice pay raise to $1,600 a year—the most he would ever earn in one year.

In 1867, Whitman published the fourth edition of *Leaves of Grass*, the first update since 1860. It was his edits to this version that had gotten Whitman fired from the Bureau of Indian Affairs two years before. This edition was widely circulated in Europe, enhancing Whitman's reputation as America's poet.

Whitman turned into a sort of reactionary against the Radical Republicans, defending President Andrew Johnson (Lincoln's successor) and opposing his impeachment. Johnson did little to support Reconstruction or to help the freed slaves. He pardoned thousands of Confederate leaders, something that Whitman saw firsthand through his job in the Attorney General's Office. When Johnson fired Secretary of War Edwin Stanton in February 1868, Congress impeached the president. Whitman attended part of the proceedings. The Senate acquitted Johnson by just one vote in May, but his presidency was finished.[224]

As the country sought a new president to replace Johnson in November 1868, all eyes turned toward Ulysses S. Grant, the general who had won

The Freedman's Bank building, where Whitman worked in 1870–71. *Library of Congress.*

the Civil War. Whitman was tepid about Grant. "The Republicans have exploited the negro too intensely, & there comes a reaction," Walt wrote. "But that is going to be provided for. According to present appearances the good, worthy, non-demonstrative, average-representing Grant will be chosen President next fall." Grant won the presidency without Walt's vote.[225]

On July 1, 1870, the Department of Justice was created. The attorney general was tasked with leading the new department, and Whitman became one of its first employees. The next year, his office moved out of the Treasury Building to the new Freedman's Bank Building across Pennsylvania Avenue (now part of the Treasury Annex). However, Whitman didn't stay long at the new location. On January 1, 1872, he transferred to the Office of the Solicitor of the Treasury, and he moved back into the Treasury Building. It was there that Whitman suffered his stroke a year later.

Having served much of his time as a federal clerk during the Grant administration, Whitman ultimately became a Grant supporter and, likewise, eventually came around to supporting the constitutional amendments that protected African American rights. He wrote to his mother, "I saw Grant to-day on the avenue walking by himself—(I always salute him, & he does the same to me.)"[226] Two weeks before the 1872 election, Walt published an unsigned op-ed in the *Evening Star*, placing himself among the very diverse audience that stopped to laugh at Thomas Nast's latest political cartoons, which were hung in storefronts. "Among the rest of the jolly heads in one group on the Avenue, we saw the white locks and red face of Walt Whitman, proving that he can, on due provocation, laugh enormously, (notwithstanding some of his foreign critics,) and was now doing the same," as Whitman described himself in the third person.[227]

During his final years in Washington, Whitman witnessed the city transform from a dusty, muddy backwater into an elegant urban center. President Grant established territorial government, a version of home rule, in 1870 and appointed Henry D. Cooke as the first governor, followed by Alexander "Boss" Shepherd. The city was transformed with public works—the streets were paved, the putrid Washington City Canal was filled in and paved over as Constitution Avenue and streetlights were installed. The heavy spending bankrupted the city, and territorial government came to an end in 1874.

Chapter 11
DEMOCRATIC VISTAS

A lthough writers often have the reputation for being solitary—and
Whitman was no exception—Walt could be gregarious around
intimate friends. He became part of a literary circle in Washington, one
that was altogether healthier than his earlier circle at Pfaff's in Manhattan.
The members were government clerks rather than bohemians, and they
provided a more stable foundation of friendship that would likewise help
Whitman's career.

The post–Civil War Walt Whitman was far less naïve than the poet who
had published *Leaves of Grass* in the 1850s. The war changed him. It also
renewed him and gave his life a new purpose beyond literature, though he
would continually strive to be America's great poet. Literary critic Harold
Bloom believes that Whitman's greatest era as a poet was 1855 to 1865.
He wrote, "After 1865, the sane and sacred Whitman burned out. He had
nursed one too many dying young soldier, and discovered that in elegizing
Lincoln he had elegized his own poetic vocation."[228]

Yet Whitman had many more lines of verse in him, much of it good, and
he would eventually turn to prose to write about his Civil War experiences.
Although his wartime poetry isn't considered as ingenious as the first three
editions of *Leaves of Grass*, it sealed his reputation as the poet laureate of the
Civil War.

WHITMAN'S CIRCLE OF FRIENDS

Like many transplants to Washington, Whitman already knew a number of people from his days in Brooklyn and Boston, including Charles Eldridge and William Douglas O'Connor. Having two literary friends helped introduce him to other like-minded people who were the core of his life in Washington.

One of Walt's most eccentric acquaintances was Count Adam Gurowski, a fiery one-eyed Polish exile and radical. They had met at Pfaff's in Manhattan. William O'Connor, who translated some of the count's papers into English, described him as "a madman with lucid intervals."[229] Yet Gurowski appreciated Whitman and was one of his vocal defenders, especially after Walt was fired from the Bureau of Indian Affairs, and Walt seemed rather fond of the man. Gurowski published a three-volume diary of the Civil War that included three categories of men: Praise, Half and Half and Blame. Walt merited the Praise column, as did Abraham Lincoln. "He knew every thing & growled & found fault with everybody—but was always very courteous to me," Walt wrote to his brother Jeff. Gurowski died in May 1866, and Walt attended the funeral in Congressional Cemetery. "His funeral was simple but very impressive—all the big radicals were there."[230]

Another New York acquaintance was William Swinton. He was the brother of Walt's friend John Swinton, editor of the *New York Times*. William served as a war correspondent for the *Times*, although he told Union authorities that he was writing a history of the war. His journalism was considered unscrupulous. General Grant suspected that Swinton was feeding information to the Confederates. Swinton barely escaped a firing squad in 1864 when Grant ordered him released but banned him from the front.[231] Walt had a low opinion of Swinton's journalism, as he wrote to his mother: "I do not always depend on Swinton's accounts [in the *Times*]—I think he is apt to make things full as bad as they are, if not worse."[232]

Walt recalled taking a long hike with Swinton and then dining at the Willard Hotel afterward. Both men were famished. "We ordered some meat. The waiter brought a piece for me not larger than a big thumb. I could have eaten a dozen its size," Walt said.

Swinton asked indignantly, "Is that all you have?"

The waiter answered, "Oh no! We have plenty outside," the waiter answered.

"Bring us in all you have!" Swinton demanded, stunning the waiter with their prodigious appetites.[233] Swinton went on to have a few legendary drinking bouts with Mark Twain and later moved to California.

Walt's closest friends were settled with families. Most weekday evenings, Whitman ventured to the home of Nelly and William O'Connor, who hosted the literary circle. The O'Connors had a bustling salon filled with Washington notables like John and Ursula Burroughs and Charles Eldridge. Occasional visitors to the circle included poets John and Sarah Piatt (John was the librarian of the House of Representatives), Assistant Attorney General Hubley Ashton and many others.

Doubtless, Walt's friends knew of his relationship with Peter Doyle; in fact, John Burroughs, Charles Eldridge and the O'Connors knew him well. Burroughs described the "unlettered car-driver" as "a kind of 'mute inglorious' Whitman, and a manly and lovable character."[234]

A portrait of Walt Whitman, taken by Frank Pearsall in 1869, when Whitman was fifty. *Library of Congress.*

Nelly O'Connor recalled winter nights when Walt would enter with a bottle of whiskey, a lemon and some sugar and oversee the production of hot toddies, down to the moment when the water should be removed from the heat. Walt was precise and exact in his instructions (Nelly was a good cook and probably knew how to make a toddy without Walt's help—it's an easy recipe). And this was from a man who typically served his tea in the same tin cup that he boiled the water in and who ate his own cooking on a shingle, as he owned no plates.[235]

Grace Channing, the O'Connors' niece, witnessed the literary circle as a child and marveled at the depth and range of conversation:

> *Conversation cannot have gone beyond that—before or since. It was not the Brahminical cult but the Olympian. One sign of it was the laughter; I have never heard such gaiety, such arrows of wit struck everywhere, and nothing and nobody was exempt. Governments, creeds, and civilizations*

were dealt with without remorse. Nothing that man had ever done or might attempt to do was left untouched. It was there I learned the boundless spaces of thought,—what a free mind means. Science, art, government, ethics, cultural values. And it was not one night—but every.[236]

Charles Eldridge remembered Whitman's decade in Washington: "During that period we met at O'Connor's house every night for months at a time with hardly a break, and we talked of everything that the human mind could conceive. I have often wished that I had kept a diary, or at a least a memorandum of some of these memorable conversations. Walt was then in the prime of his splendid manhood and O'Connor was the most brilliant talker I have ever heard or expect to hear."[237]

Nelly fondly remembered the nightly gatherings and how the conversation whirled around the topics of the day. Like Eldridge, she had but one regret:

I wish I had some record of the talks, discussions, arguments, that were nightly indulged in. No notes were taken, for all were engaged more or less in the mêlée, and no one could dream how valuable such notes might have been as future reminders...Philosophy, history, religion, literature,—authors, ancient and modern,—language, music, and every possible question as to the conduct of the Civil War,—everything was discussed, and every side was heard.[238]

On Sunday mornings, Whitman had breakfast at the Capitol Hill home of John and Ursula Burroughs (377 First Street East, now the site of the Russell Senate Office Building). Whitman was seldom on time, Burroughs noted.

Walt was usually late for breakfast, and Ursula, who was as punctual as the clock, would get in a pucker. The coffee would boil, the griddle would smoke, and car after car would go jingling by, but no Walt. The situation at times verged on the tragic. But at last a car would stop, and Walt would roll off it and saunter up to the door—so cheery, and so unaware of the annoyance he had caused, that we soon forgot our ill-humor.[239]

The Washington and Georgetown streetcar—Peter Doyle's employer—ran past the house, which was how Walt got to the Burroughs home. Nelly O'Connor described Walt as having "a slow-moving, rather lethargic body," and the same might be said of his habits: he was perpetually late, preferring spontaneity over a rigid schedule.[240]

In 1867, Burroughs moved to a new house at 1332 V Street Northwest (or 1330 or 1336, depending on which version of *Boyd's City Directory* you consult). It was close to Fourteenth Street and a horsecar line that took him downtown to work at the Treasury Building. That same year, Burroughs published *Notes on Walt Whitman as Poet and Person*, the first biography about Walt. Burroughs allowed Whitman to write portions of the book. Burroughs might have been the poet's friend, yet he privately questioned many of Walt's writings. His biography wasn't written with the same strident enthusiasm that O'Connor had shown a year earlier in *The Good Gray Poet*. Burroughs produced an expanded second edition in 1872.

"I should describe him, off-hand, as a cheerful, rather quiet man, easily pleased with others, letting them do most of the talking, seeking not the least conquest or display," Burroughs wrote about Walt. He added, "The 'eccentricity' of Walt Whitman, though it has been part of the material of many a paragraphist and magazine writer for the last ten years, has not a particle of real foundation."[241]

Walt had close contacts with the local Washington press, especially with Stuart Crosby Noyes, publisher of the *Evening Star*. When the *Star* ran a front-page overview of literary life among the federal clerks in 1868, Whitman garnered half the article's length while William Douglas O'Connor earned just a small paragraph. The author's article went by the penname "Judson" of the *Raleigh (NC) Standard* and claimed to have known Walt for six years. The description of Whitman's habits and personality is uncanny—so much that one suspects that Walt had a hand in writing his section. "He looks more like a thoughtful mechanic or boatman than like a grand poet or capable clerk. He dresses coarsely; his hair and beard, almost white, grows wild about his neck and face, and though his appearance is wierd [*sic*] and unusual, he always attracts shy children and shrinking natures, and to know him is to love him," Judson (or, perhaps, Walt) wrote. In newspaper articles Whitman published about himself anonymously, he often stressed his appearance, clothing and sunburnt features, and this article was no different. The *Star* called Whitman "the best abused man in the country," a crown of martyrdom that the poet gladly wore.[242]

DEMOCRATIC VISTAS

In 1871, Whitman published the fifth edition of *Leaves of Grass*, writing in the preface that this would be the last edition (it wasn't). That same year, he published *Democratic Vistas*, his most passionate treatise. *Democratic Vistas* voiced Whitman's disapproval of the country's postwar trajectory. America was rife with the corruption and greed of the Gilded Age, and its citizenry wanted nothing more than crass materialism. "Never was there, perhaps, more hollowness at heart than at present, and here in the United States. Genuine belief seems to have left us," he wrote. "The spectacle is appaling [*sic*]. We are living in an atmosphere of hypocrisy throughout."[243]

"In business, (this all-devouring modern word, business,) the one sole object is, by any means, pecuniary gain," Whitman continued. "The best class we show, is but a mob of fashionably dress'd speculators and vulgarians."[244] One sees in Whitman's prose his propensity for making lists and writing run-on sentences with far too many commas and phrases.

So what was Whitman's solution to the moral crisis of the 1870s? Literature. "Two or three really original American poets...would give more compaction and more moral identity, (the quality to-day most needed) to these States, than all its Constitutions, legislative and judicial ties," he prophesied."[245] "Immortal Judah lives, and Greece immortal lives, in a couple of poems."[246] Yet it was also the equivalent of arguing that rock-and-roll could save the world, when in fact it couldn't. In *Democratic Vistas*, Whitman played the visionary, but he offered no practical recommendations.

Whitman claimed, rather extravagantly, that "America has yet morally and artistically originated nothing."[247] He called for literature that would unite the nation. He seemed blind, or somehow unaware, of the national literature emerging all around him among his contemporaries: Alcott, Emerson, Hawthorne, Howells, James, Melville, Poe, Stowe, Thoreau and Twain—and Whitman himself. This was a dual-purposed theme that Whitman repeated throughout his career: that his poems could spark national unity and that America ignored its greatest writers. Neither was essentially true.

"After All, Not to Create Only"

Although Whitman railed against Gilded Age greed, he marveled at the industrial and technological changes that were overtaking the country as much as he was smitten by the working-class men who worked at these factories. He witnessed the Industrial Revolution in Brooklyn and saw firsthand the industries in the nation's capital at the Washington Arsenal, the Navy Yard and the factories of Georgetown. It was nothing short of wondrous.

Walt composed a number of poems that showed his appreciation for how industry and technological change could bring the world together, including "Passage to India," published in 1871, two years after the opening of the Suez Canal and the transcontinental railroad. That same year, the American Institute invited Whitman to read a poem at the fortieth National Industrial Exposition in New York. Whitman crafted a new poem, officially known as "Song of the Exposition" but better known as "After All, Not to Create Only." He recited it publicly on September 7. It praised the technological innovation that was rapidly changing American life:

> *By thud of machinery and shrill steam-whistle undismay'd*
> *Bluff'd not by a bit of drain-pipe, gasometers, artificial fertilizers,*
> *Smiling and pleas'd with palpable intent to stay,*
> *She's here, install'd amid the kitchen ware!*

Walt wired the poem to the *Evening Star*, which printed it on the front page that same day, as if to demonstrate how technology could deliver news in real time.[248] He also published a favorable anonymous review of his reading at the Industrial Exposition in the *Washington Chronicle*. Whitman was someone who sought national recognition for his poetry. He wanted people to buy and read his works, and he wanted to be highly regarded as a poet. Walt understood the need for good public relations—even if he had to engage in subterfuge. Good reviews directly translated into sales.[249]

The poem was widely distributed and contributed to Whitman's growing fame. The line "After all, not to create only" became a favorite of congressman, Civil War general and future president James Garfield. Peter Doyle described their walks along Pennsylvania Avenue when they would run into the congressman:

> *Garfield and Walt were very good friends. Garfield had a large manly voice; we would be going along the Avenue together—Walt and me—and we would hear Garfield's salutation at the rear. He always signaled Walt with the cry: "After all not to create only!" When we heard that we always knew who was coming. Garfield would catch up and they would enter into a talk; I would fall back sometimes. They spoke of books*

Congressman (and later president) James Garfield was one of
Whitman's friends. He would greet Whitman with, "After all, not to
create only!" *Library of Congress.*

*mainly but of every other earthly thing also. Often they would not get
through the first run and would go up and down the Avenue several times
together—I was out of it.*[250]

One wonders if Doyle found this annoying or if he was just being tolerant.
Pete might have felt outclassed by Whitman's friends, or he might have felt
that Walt was just being Walt, that his partner simply enjoyed having urbane
conversations about literature.

THE CASE OF OFFICER DOYLE

Peter Doyle's eldest brother, Francis Michael, was a police officer in Washington's Metropolitan Police Department. The police department had been created in 1861, the year that the Civil War began. Like Pete, Francis was born in Ireland, but while Pete served in the Confederate army, Francis remained loyal to the Union. He enlisted in the army and then served in the navy for two years (1865–67) aboard USS *Wasp*. He joined the MPD in 1868.[251]

In May 1871, a man named Burnham asked a police court judge to issue a warrant for the arrest of a five year-old boy, John Muretete (or Muretet or Murete-let, as conflicting newspapers spelled it), for stealing nine eggs from his shanty on the Ellipse. Francis Doyle was ordered to execute the warrant. Against his better judgment, he went to the child's home that evening, found him asleep in bed and arrested him. Muretete stayed the night in the police station. The next morning, a judge promptly released the boy.

An intense public outcry of police brutality arose against Doyle for arresting the child, and the episode proved embarrassing to the police department. On May 17, the police commissioners charged Doyle with cruelty and bad judgment. They found that Doyle's conduct was unbecoming for a police officer and ruled that he would be "severely reprimanded"—which is to say, given a slap on the wrist. He continued serving on the police force.[252]

Angered at the injustice to his partner's brother, Walt drafted an op-ed defending Francis's conduct. "As to Doyle, he is an energetic officer, a little stern perhaps; for he has been kept on duty in 'Hooker's Division [Washington's red-light district];' but he bears an excellent reputation and served the Union cause, as soldier or sailor, all through the war," Walt wrote. He never published the opinion piece.[253] The case showed how close Walt was to the Doyle family and that he knew Francis and held him in high regard.

Two months after the incident, Doyle was charged with assault on a woman who was likely a prostitute while he attempted to arrest her. The case was immediately dropped, however, when one of the witnesses changed the story originally told.[254]

Francis Doyle's service in the police department tragically came to an end on December 29, 1871. Accompanied by two fellow policemen, he went to execute a warrant to arrest John Shea at his home on Maryland Avenue Southwest. Shea was a notorious fencer of stolen goods. He had bought a stolen watch, and the owner had traced it to him, leading to the arrest warrant. John was not home, but his fiery wife, Mary, was. The confrontation turned violent. When the officers attempted to enter the house, Mary warned them to leave or she would shoot them with a pistol. As they forced their way through the door, she fired, mortally wounding Doyle in the chest. He was the first MPD officer to be killed in the line of duty.[255]

Francis Doyle was thirty-eight years old at the time of his death. He left behind his widow, Eleanor; three children; and a home at 340 K Street Southwest. The funeral was held at St. Dominic Church on the last day of 1871, and then fifty-two policemen escorted Francis's remains for burial in Congressional Cemetery.[256] Walt attended the funeral with the Doyle family.[257]

Mary Shea was brought up on murder charges (later reduced to manslaughter), and John Shea was charged with buying stolen property. He was acquitted in March 1872. At Mary's two-day trial the following month, the jury deliberated for fifty minutes and concluded that it was an accident. She was found not guilty. Mary returned home a free woman, though there were many—especially in the police community—who presumed her guilt.[258]

WHITMAN'S GROWING POETIC REPUTATION

Walt was clearly on the nation's literary map by the early 1870s. Part of his 1871 version of "Song of Myself" was included in *The Poets and Poetry of America.*[259] However, Ralph Waldo Emerson excluded Whitman from his 1874 poetry anthology *Parnassus.* Their friendship seems to have faded, and Emerson had possibly concluded that Whitman had used him one too many times.

The Washington hometown press came to appreciate Whitman, often publicizing his new works, his trips to visit his mother and, later, his health concerns. With that said, the *Evening Star* wasn't always sure what to make of Walt.

> *Then beside, to be candid, Walt Whitman is a pretty hard nut to crack. His involved sentences always hiding at least half their meaning, his kangaroo leaps as if from one crag to another, his appalling catalogues, (enough to stagger the bravest heart,) his unheard of demand for brains in the reader as well as the thing read, and then his scornful silence, never explaining anything nor answering any attack, all lay him fairly open to be misunderstood, to slur, burlesque, and sometimes spiteful innuendo; and will probably always continue to do so.*[260]

In March 1871, there was a false report of Whitman's death in a railroad accident. The *New York World* prematurely published a two-column obituary for the poet, which the *Evening Star* editors thoroughly enjoyed taking to task. The *World* "declines to publish any more obituaries of people who are not 'reliably dead.'" The *World* need not on that account hesitate to publish the obituary of the Tammany Ring," as Boss Tweed had been taken down the year before. In fact, New York's Tammany Hall machine would live on.[261]

Walt visited New York in February and March 1872, an unusual time for him. It was part vacation but part business. He was working on a reprint of the 1871 edition of *Leaves of Grass*. He passed through New York three months later on his way to deliver his first poetry reading at a university.

Whitman was invited to read a poem for the June 26 commencement at Dartmouth College at the request of the students, who possibly wanted to irk the faculty. He composed and read "As a Strong Bird on Pinions Free." Repeating the publicity tactic that he had used the previous year for the Industrial Exposition, he critiqued his public performance in the *New York Herald*, an article that he wrote in the third person to disguise that it was written by the poet himself. "He was very easy in his manner of delivery and evinced an unusual degree of what might be called, in a word, emphasis, but outwardly he shows perfect nonchalance. His vitality and electricity are in the voice, which, although not starling and loud, is impressive and animating, almost beyond example," Walt wrote, as if advertising his voice for future paid speaking engagements. "His inherent intellectual animation is probably beyond that of any speaker of the age," he concluded. Whitman was already a nationally recognized poet, yet he still felt compelled to self-aggrandize.[262]

The *Evening Star* echoed the refrain, thanks to Walt's friendship with publisher Crosby Stuart Noyes, and one suspects that Walt had his hand in its review of the Dartmouth reading. Whitman "avowedly views the whole tribe of poets and novelists with contempt," the newspaper recorded. "Current art, poetry and ecclesiasticism, however serviceable for their time in Europe and the past, are impotent in America, and incompatible with her genius."[263]

After the Dartmouth commencement, Walt traveled throughout New England on this two-month trip, seeing his neurotic sister Hannah in Burlington, Vermont, for the last time. He would financially support her and her husband, landscape painter Charles Heyde, whom he detested, for the rest of his life. (This means that Whitman took a total of four months off from his federal position in 1872 for literary endeavors.) The summer was quite hot. Walt always had difficulty with the heat, and upon returning to Washington, he was ill for almost a week.

The Breaking of the Discipleship

Though Whitman had long stood against slavery, he had a more uncomfortable relationship when it came to the question of black civil rights. Like many whites of the era, he hated slavery because it competed with white labor. Charles Eldridge related Walt's racial views for the *New York Times* in 1902: "Of the negro race he had a poor opinion. He said that there was in the constitution of the negro's mind an irredeemable trifling or volatile element, and he would never amount to much in the scale of civilization. I never knew him to have a friend among the negroes while he was in Washington, and he never seemed to care for them or they for him, although he never manifested any particular aversion to them."[264]

In his 1871 essay *Democratic Vistas*, Whitman touched on racial undertones. He had serious reservations about extending the vote to African American men, which the Fifteenth Amendment had recently guaranteed. "I will not gloss over the appaling [*sic*] dangers of universal suffrage in the United States," he wrote.[265] Walt would likewise question women's suffrage. He supported human dignity for all, but Whitman was no radical.

Whitman and O'Connor differed greatly in their opinion of blacks, and they often quarreled. Their friendship ruptured in 1872 over the question of black suffrage. O'Connor had been a radical abolitionist and was a proponent of black political rights. John Burroughs, who witnessed the fight, described it years later:

> O'Connor became enraged at what Walt said about the unfitness of the negroes for voting. They were in a habit of goring each other in argument like two bulls, and that time Walt was, I guess, rather brutal and insulting. It was in O'Connor's home. O'Connor fired up and turned on him. Walt took his hat and went home in a pet. Then when they met on the street the next day, Walt put out his hand; but William shied around and went past. The iron had entered his soul.[266]

O'Connor was so angry with Whitman that he couldn't forgive him. With that, Walt lost his greatest literary champion. O'Connor also broke with his wife; he and Nelly soon separated. Grace Channing, O'Connor's niece, wrote about the argument:

> *No group of people could continue forever to play with explosives without a casualty. And given the magnitude of the two involved, it was bound to be a fatality as well. Whitman was arrogant; my uncle was proud as he was generous. He had literally spent himself upon Whitman; something the latter said outraged him. Whitman rose and took his hat and departed. My aunt took his part. Whereupon my uncle took his hat and departed.*[267]

O'Connor may have come to realize that his wife, Nelly, was in love with Walt, and when she took his side in the argument over the black vote, he felt it was a double betrayal.

In January 1873, John Burroughs moved back to New York after more than nine years in Washington, leaving his wife, Ursula, behind temporarily while he got settled. "My greatest loss will be in you, my dear Walt, but then I shall look forward to having you up here a good long time at a stretch, which will be better than the crumbs I used to get of you in W[ashington]," Burroughs wrote.[268] Although their friendship continued long distance, Whitman had lost two key allies in one season: John Burroughs and William O'Connor. It was the unwinding of a literary circle that had lasted a decade. Walt would never have such a support group again. And he soon suffered a stroke that would forever change his life.

Chapter 12

THE GOOD GRAY POET

A s Whitman's recognition spread, he adopted two important myths about himself that he would carry for the rest of his life. The first, as we've seen, was the myth of the Good Gray Poet, propagated by William Douglas O'Connor with his book of the same name. It transformed Whitman from "one of the roughs" into a wise sage.

The other myth of Whitman's later life was that he was a neglected poet, that he had many fans in Europe but was largely ignored in the United States. He conveyed a sense of martyrdom. This was patently untrue: he was frequently published, and although he didn't earn the sums of money that novelists such as Mark Twain did (poetry has always been a rather non-lucrative niche in the United States), he did earn decent money from his writing, especially in his later years, when he earned commissions for poems and speeches.

THE STROKE

Whitman often suffered headaches, a fullness in his head and dizzy spells. He often blamed this on the weather, especially as his symptoms worsened in the heat. These were symptoms, in fact, of hypertension, exacerbated by his being overweight. And it wasn't in the heat of summer that his illness would strike.

By 1873, Walt was living at 535 Fifteenth Street Northwest, a cold garret apartment right across the street from his office in the Treasury Building. Since his room was unheated, he often went to the office on weekends or stayed late in the evenings to keep warm on cold days. Whitman was reading at his desk on the night of Thursday, January 23, when he suffered a stroke. He somehow made his way home, climbed the steps to his attic room and crawled into bed. He awoke the next morning and found himself partly paralyzed. Friends discovered him there late in the morning.

Walt's circle of friends rallied to help the stricken poet. Peter Doyle, Charles Eldridge and Nelly O'Connor visited Whitman and attended to him, and many others called on him. But they weren't nurses, and Walt needed more help. Medicine of the day offered little for stroke victims, and though Walt's condition was stable, he didn't improve. He could only walk short distances, and his left leg was nearly useless.

Peter Doyle was now working for the Baltimore & Potomac Railroad as a brakeman and sat with Walt before his evening shift began. A decade later, Walt inscribed a copy of *Specimen Days* for Doyle, remembering how vital it was for Pete just to be there when Walt was ill. It was a reversal for Walt, who had sat by the bedside of thousands of young soldiers.

> *Pete do you remember—(of course you do—I do well)—those great long jovial walks we had at times for years, (1866–'72) out of Washington City—often moonlight nights, 'way to "Good Hope"; or, Sundays, up and down the Potomac shores, one side or the other, sometimes ten miles at a stretch? Or when you work'd on the horse-cars, and I waited for you, coming home late together—or resting and chatting at the Market, corner 7th street and the Avenue, and eating those nice musk or water melons? Or during my tedious sickness and first paralysis ('73) how you used to come to my solitary garret room and make up my bed, and enliven me and chat for an hour or so—or perhaps go out and get the medicines Dr. Drinkard had order'd for me—before you went on duty?*[269]

One day a prominent visitor dropped by Whitman's garret: British novelist Edmund Yates. Overruling Pete's objections, Whitman allowed the man in. "No two men were ever different," Pete recalled. "Yates elegant, dressy, cultured—Walt plain, sick in bed, his room all littered and poor. But both men were perfectly at home. Yates did not seem fazed, Walt never was."[270]

Tragic news arrived in February when Walt learned that his beloved sister-in-law Mattie, Jeff's wife, had died in St. Louis. This was a significant loss for Walt, as he was very close to the woman and had written her many letters.

John Burroughs stopped by Washington briefly in March, probably to finish the family's move to New York, and paid a visit to Whitman. On April 30, Walt wrote to Burroughs, explaining how much he missed their family: "If I could just get 'round to sit an hour or so for a change, and chat with 'Sula and you, two or three times a week, I believe it would do me good—but I must take it out in imagination."[271]

WHITMAN LEAVES WASHINGTON

The previous summer, Walt's mother, Louisa, and mentally disabled brother, Eddy, moved in with George Whitman and his family in Camden, New Jersey. Louisa's health was failing, and she had long suffered from rheumatism. With her departure from Brooklyn, the two-century line of Whitmans on Long Island came to an end. As she declined, George summoned Walt to Camden in May. They didn't have much time.

On May 16, shortly before departing to visit his mother, Whitman signed a will, naming his brother George as executor. Although he left most of his money to his mother (who would die exactly a week later), Walt left eighty-nine dollars to Peter Doyle to pay a debt, as well as his silver watch. "I wish it given to him, with my love," he wrote.[272] Walt

Walt Whitman's mother, Louisa Van Velsor Whitman (1795–1873). *Library of Congress.*

was still quite ill, but he attended to his mother for the last three days of her life. She died on May 23—exactly four months after Walt's stroke. She was seventy-eight.

Louisa's death was as devastating to Walt as his stroke was. There was no one in the world he was closer to than his mother. Faced with not only physical debilitation, he also became depressed. Charles Eldridge wrote to John Burroughs of their friend's deteriorating condition after Louisa's funeral:

> Walt returned here about a week after the funeral in a very depressed condition and complaining more in regard to himself than I have ever heard him do since he got sick…He still has those distressed spells in the head quite often, and his locomotion is no better…The fact is, I begin to doubt whether Walt is going to recover, and I am very apprehensive of another attack…He is a mere physical wreck to what he was…It is a terrible misfortune, one of the saddest spectacles I have ever seen…Such vigor, health, and endurance to be so changed, is a melancholy thing; and if it should continue for any length of time, I think it would prey upon his spirits and make him hypochondriacal [sic].[273]

Whitman's recovery was very slow. The stroke hadn't impacted his speech, but he had a terrible time walking more than a short distance; plus, his left leg would be lame for the rest of his life. After his mother's funeral, Walt returned to Washington on June 2. Unable to live in his walk-up garret anymore, he moved into Hubley Ashton's mansion. He stayed there two weeks and then, in mid-June, decided to leave Washington for good. He moved in with his brother George. Whitman lived in Camden for the rest of his life.

Walt resided with George's family for the next eleven years, finally moving out in 1884 when he got his own residence at 330 Mickle Street. Other than his brother's family, he initially knew no one in Camden and was quite isolated, though he soon began to make friends.

Whitman's move to Camden transformed his relationship with Peter Doyle into a long-distance one. Shortly after moving in with his brother's family, he wrote a letter of distress: "Pete, I am not having a very good time—my head troubles me—yesterday was as bad as ever—as far from well as ever."[274] A month later, Walt signaled that their future together was in doubt. On July 24, he noted that his health had hardly improved and that he had little room for optimism: "I still think I shall get over this, and we will be together again and have some good times—but for all that it is best for you to be prepared for something different—my strength can't

A signed 1873 carte de visite of Walt Whitman, taken in Philadelphia, reinforced Walt's image as the Good Gray Poet. The butterfly, made of cardboard, was tied on his finger. *Library of Congress.*

stand the pull forever, and if continued must sooner or later give out."[275]

Pete came to visit on occasion (Walt wrote to Nelly O'Connor about Pete's visit in May 1874: "What good it did me!"),[276] but their romantic relationship would not be the same. It trailed off, though they continued to write for many years. Pete kept all of Walt's letters, but sadly, Walt didn't do the same. Whitman purged some of his correspondence late in life, concerned about his public image if they should ever be published. It makes Walt's letters to Pete seem one-sided. Correspondence is an ongoing conversation, and yet we only have half of it.

Absent from the federal workforce, Walt hired a substitute, Walter Godey, in August 1873. However, as Walt's health didn't improve enough for him to return to work, he was discharged from government service the next year. He was now a disabled man without a reliable source of income, other than the occasional royalty, though he did have room and board from George's family. Walt suffered another stroke in February 1875, two years after the first.

Whitman returned to Washington only once, in November 1875, on a side tour from a trip to Baltimore for the dedication of a monument to Edgar Allan Poe. He stayed with Peter Doyle's aunt and uncle, Ann and Michael Nash, whom he counted among his close friends, and paid a visit to Nelly O'Connor. He never visited Washington again.

WHITMAN'S POSTERITY

After his strokes, Whitman wrote little great poetry but instead reshuffled and revisited his existing works. He published narratives like *Memoranda During the War* and *Specimen Days* that repackaged material he had already written. Many argue that his most creative period ended with the Civil War in 1865. *Memoranda* was largely a collection of *New York Times* articles that Whitman republished in the *New York Weekly Graphic* in 1874 and then self-published in a book two years later. He printed only about one hundred copies.

We see Walt's concern for posterity in *Memoranda*. Thirteen years after publishing an article in the *New York Times*, Whitman appended his statement about seeing President Lincoln everyday with this sentence: "We have got so that we always exchange bows, and very cordial ones." We don't know if Lincoln and Whitman actually exchanged bows, only that it was important for Whitman to establish some kind of recognition from the president. This was part of Walt's occasional forays into altering, embellishing and revising the record for posterity's sake.

In February 1876, Whitman published his account of Lincoln's assassination in the *New York Sun*. "Walt was not at the theatre the night Lincoln was shot," Peter Doyle later remarked. "It was me he got all that from in the book—they are almost my words."[277] Three years later, Whitman gave the first of his nearly annual "Death of Abraham Lincoln" lectures, a popular speech about Lincoln's assassination. He capped the evening by reading "O Captain! My Captain!" As the curtain fell, a little girl would come on stage and hand Walt a bouquet of lilacs to enhance the drama. One came away with the sense that Walt had witnessed the assassination when, in fact, he was in Brooklyn at the time. The lecture was always well attended and a source of considerable income for Whitman.

In 1879, Walt visited his brother Jeff, who was superintendent of the waterworks in St. Louis, and saw many of the western states for the first time. The next year, he traveled to Canada to visit Maurice Bucke, one of his devotees. Peter Doyle joined them at Niagara Falls and accompanied him back to Philadelphia. Walt also traveled numerous times to visit John and Ursula Burroughs on their farm in upstate New York. Burroughs remained Walt's friend until the end, their friendship lasting nearly three decades.

Whitman mourned the loss of his good friend President James Garfield, who was assassinated by Charles Guiteau in 1881 at the Baltimore and Potomac Railroad station in Washington. The attending physician was the same Dr. Willard Bliss from Armory Square Hospital. Garfield died more than two months after being shot after his wounds became infected as the medical community argued over how best to treat the president. Walt published "The Sobbing of the Bells" in Garfield's honor.

Whitman was a poet, but his cohort of increasingly international followers saw him as a prophet, one whose writings would replace the Bible as a new religion. This obviously did not happen, and Whitman today is remembered simply as an outstanding poet. Over the years, he had many visitors in Camden, most famously Oscar Wilde.

Walt produced a sixth edition of *Leaves of Grass* in 1881. This was only the second time that the poetry volume had an actual publisher (the first was in 1860). Four months after its publication, the Boston district attorney, Oliver Stephens, demanded that the book be withdrawn for obscenity. Whitman refused to remove the offending poems, and so the publisher ended the book's run. But that wasn't the end of the edition—far from it.

William Douglas O'Connor—who hadn't spoken with Walt since they broke off their friendship in 1872—came to Walt's defense. The mild

uproar over this show of Comstockery benefited Whitman immensely. Walt liked to play the maligned, martyred poet, but he had also come to appreciate that controversy sells. A Philadelphia publisher took on the project, and the sixth edition continued to sell. Whitman later praised O'Connor: "He was a born sample here in the 19th century of the flower and symbol of olden time first class knighthood. Thrice blessed be his memory!"[278]

William Douglas O'Connor in 1885. *Library of Congress.*

The 1881 edition of *Leaves of Grass* sealed Whitman's reputation as America's foremost poet, and it brought him a measure of financial security that he had never experienced before. Whitman had been publishing—often self-publishing—poetry for nearly three decades before he had seen such commercial success. The next year, he followed the volume with his autobiography, *Specimen Days*, which sold well.

The health of Whitman's literary champion, William O'Connor, soon began to decline, and he moved back in with Nelly, who nursed him. He died on May 9, 1889, and was buried in Washington's Oak Hill Cemetery. Walt turned seventy that month. Walt's closest brother, Jeff, died in St. Louis the next year.

With Peter Doyle far away in Washington, Walt found a series of young men in Camden who caught his eye. Henry Stafford was one such fellow. Whitman had left his silver watch to Doyle in his 1873 will, but it would actually go to Stafford. Another devoted young disciple, Horace Traubel, began interviewing Whitman in 1888 and took extensive notes of their conversations. He later published nine volumes of transcripts called *With Walt Whitman in Camden*. Several strokes in 1888 left Whitman further debilitated and wheelchair bound.

When Doyle's mother, Catherine, died in 1885, Pete moved to Philadelphia. However, Pete saw little of Walt his last few years—the two men had lost touch.[279] Pete spoke with some remorse when confronted about this fact: "I know he wondered why I saw so little of him the three or four years before he died, but when I explained it to him he understood...It was only this: In the old days I always had open doors to Walt—going, coming, staying, as I chose. Now, I had to run the gauntlet of Mrs. [Mary] Davis [Walt's housekeeper and housemate] and a nurse and what not. Somehow I could not do it."

"We loved each other deeply," Pete said. "Walt realized I never swerved from him—he knows it now—that is enough."[280] Pete might have been dancing around the "what not," which probably referred to the two men who interviewed him: Maurice Bucke and Horace Traubel. Traubel, in particular, was encamped at Whitman's house virtually every day for the final four years of Walt's life. He had supplanted Pete in Walt's life, though not romantically. Pete was no intellectual. He may have felt outclassed by Traubel, though the men were friendly to each other.

In 1891, Whitman published the "deathbed" edition of *Leaves of Grass*, the seventh and final revision of his best-known work. He died on March 26, 1892, two months shy of his seventy-third birthday. Walt was buried at Harleigh Cemetery in Camden.

Walt Whitman in 1887. *Library of Congress.*

Pete Doyle came to the funeral. He was forty-nine and would never be in another relationship. He died in Philadelphia on April 19, 1907, at age sixty-three. He was buried in Congressional Cemetery near his mother and brothers, Edward and Francis. Neither Whitman nor Doyle's death notices mentioned the name of the other.[281]

Whitman began his ten years in Washington as a nearly accidental visitor who envisioned a unique role for himself in helping tens of thousands of sick and wounded Civil War soldiers. The war forever changed America, just as it did Whitman. Walt met the love of his life, Peter Doyle. He found suitable employment as a federal clerk and built a community through his literary circle. Walt won recognition as the mythical Good Gray Poet during his decade in Washington. Whitman achieved immortality through his writings, even as he elegized Abraham Lincoln in poetry.

In his poem "Song of Myself," written a decade before the Civil War ended, Walt illuminated his view of the never-ending Kosmos, the living and the dead, and his vision of immortality:

What do you think has become of the young and old men?
And what do you think has become of the women and children?

They are alive and well somewhere,
The smallest sprouts show there is really no death,
And if ever there was it led forward life, and does
not wait at the end to arrest it,
And ceas'd the moment life appear'd.

All goes onward and outward, nothing collapses,
And to die is different from what any one supposed, and luckier.

NOTES

INTRODUCTION

1. Whitman, *Memoranda*, 92.
2. Swinton, "Walt Whitman."

CHAPTER 1

3. Trowbridge, *My Own Story*, 367.
4. Burroughs, "Walt Whitman and His 'Drum Taps'."
5. Ibid., *Notes on Walt Whitman as Poet and Person*, 30–31.
6. Walt Whitman, *November Boughs*, in *Walt Whitman: Poetry and Prose*, 1,166.
7. *Critic-Record*, July 11, 1871.
8. O'Connor, *Good Gray Poet*, 31.
9. Bloom, *Walt Whitman*, 4.
10. Barrus, *Whitman and Burroughs*, xvi.
11. Ralph Waldo Emerson to Walt Whitman, July 21, 1855, in *Walt Whitman: Poetry and Prose*, 1,326.
12. Howells, *Literary Friends and Acquaintances*, 74–75.
13. Trowbridge, *My Own Story*, 362.

14. Two recent books have dealt with the question of Whitman's "lost years": Martin, *Rebel Souls*, and Genoways, *Walt Whitman and the Civil War*.
15. Whitman, *Memoranda*, 40.
16. George Washington Whitman to Thomas Jefferson Whitman, January 8, 1863, in Loving, *Civil War Letters of George Washington Whitman*, 78–79.
17. George Washington Whitman to Louisa Van Velsor Whitman, December 16, 1862, in Loving, *Civil War Letters of George Washington Whitman*, 75–76.
18. Calder, "Personal Recollections of Walt Whitman," 826.
19. Walt Whitman to Louisa Van Velson Whitman, December 29, 1862, www.whitmanarchive.org.
20. Whitman, *Memoranda*, 11.
21. Walt Whitman to Ralph Waldo Emerson, December 29, 1862, www.whitmanarchive.org.

Chapter 2

22. Walt Whitman to Louisa Van Velson Whitman, December 29, 1862, www.whitmanarchive.org.
23. Whitman, "Our National City."
24. Dickens, *American Notes and Pictures from Italy*, 138.
25. Trollope, *North America*, 301.
26. Rhodes, *All for the Union*, 20.
27. Hay, "From Washington (From Our Special Correspondent)."
28. Winkle, *Lincoln's Citadel*, xiv.
29. Alcott, *Hospital Sketches*, 18.
30. Nathaniel Hawthorne, "Chiefly About War Matters," 150–51.
31. Whitman, *Memoranda*, 113.
32. Bucke, *Calamus*, 24.
33. Whitman, "Our National City."
34. Ibid.
35. Whitman to Emerson, December 29, 1862.
36. Walt Whitman to Thomas Jefferson Whitman, February 13, 1863, www.whitmanarchive.org.
37. Grier, *Walt Whitman*, 556.
38. Ames, *Ten Years in Washington*, 437.
39. *Boyd's Washington Directory*, 1865, 90.
40. Whitman, *Memoranda*, 16.

41. Whitman, "Great Army of the Sick."
42. Roberts, "Map of Whitman's Washington Boarding Houses and Work Places," 23–28.
43. Brown, *Washington*, 315.
44. Whitman, "Our National City."

CHAPTER 3

45. Walt Whitman to Ralph Waldo Emerson, January 17, 1863, www.whitmanarchive.org.
46. Whitman, *Memoranda*, 6–7.
47. Walt Whitman, *Specimen Days*, in in *Walt Whitman: Poetry and Prose*, 778.
48. Traubel, *With Walt Whitman in Camden*, 3:293.
49. Winkle, *Lincoln's Citadel*, xiv.
50. Whitman, *Memoranda*, 46–47.
51. Whitman, "Our National City."
52. Walt Whitman to Louisa Van Velsor Whitman, June 30, 1863, www.whitmanarchive.org.
53. Whitman, *Memoranda*, 101–02.
54. Ibid., 30.
55. Walt Whitman to Louisa Van Velsor Whitman, April 15, 1863, www.whitmanarchive.org
56. Walt Whitman to Martha Whitman, January 2–4, 1863, www.whitmanarchive.org.
57. Whitman, "Great Army of the Sick."
58. Ibid., "Great Washington Hospitals."
59. Walt Whitman to Thomas Jefferson Whitman, March 6, 1863, www.whitmanarchive.org.
60. Ibid., March 18, 1863, www.whitmanarchive.org.
61. Hinton, "Washington Letter."
62. Whitman, "Our Wounded and Sick Soldiers."
63. Thomas Jefferson Whitman to Walt Whitman, February 6, 1863, www.whitmanarchive.org.
64. Walt Whitman to William S. Davis, October 1, 1863, www.whitmanarchive.org.
65. Whitman, "Great Washington Hospitals."
66. Whitman, *Memoranda*, 4.

67. Burroughs, *Notes on Walt Whitman*, 87.

68. Calder, "Personal Recollections of Walt Whitman," 831.

69. Walt Whitman to Louisa Van Velsor Whitman, March 29, 1864, www. whitmanarchive.org.

70. Whitman, *Memoranda*, 34.

71. Walt Whitman to Louisa Van Velsor Whitman, July 7, 1863, www. whitmanarchive.org.

72. Ibid., June 30, 1863, www.whitmanarchive.org.

73. Calder, "Personal Recollections of Walt Whitman," 833.

74. Whitman to Whitman, July 7, 1863.

75. Whitman, *Memoranda*, 101–02.

76. Martin G. Murray, "Specimen Days," in Kummings, *Companion to Walt Whitman*, 557–59.

CHAPTER 4

77. Whitman, *Memoranda*, 44.

78. Ibid., 90.

79. Barrus, *Whitman and Burroughs*, xxix.

80. Whitman, *Memoranda*, 71.

81. Walt Whitman to Miss Gregg, September 7, 1863, www. whitmanarchive.org.

82. Whitman, *Memoranda*, 70; see also Martin Murray, "'By Broad Potomac Shore.'"

83. Stearns, *Lady Nurse of Ward E*, 56–57.

84. Murray, "Traveling with the Wounded," www.whitmanarchive.org.

85. Walt Whitman to Mr. and Mrs. S.B. Haskell, August 10, 1863, www. whitmanarchive.org.

86. Stearns, *Lady Nurse of Ward E*, 73–74.

87. Whitman, *Memoranda*, xxxviii.

88. Calder, "Personal Recollections of Walt Whitman," 832.

89. Myerson and Shealy, *Journals of Louisa May Alcott*, 105.

90. Ibid., 116.

91. Alcott, *Hospital Sketches*, 35.

92. Ibid., 5.

93. Myerson and Shealy, *Journals of Louisa May Alcott*, 114.

94. Alcott, *Hospital Sketches*, 22.

95. Ibid., 21.
96. Ibid., 45.
97. Myerson and Shealy, *Journals of Louisa May Alcott*, 117.
98. Biographical details of Clara Barton provided by Clara Barton's Missing Soldiers Office museum, and Oates, *Woman of Valor*.

CHAPTER 5

99. Robertson, *Worshipping Walt*, 23.
100. Walt Whitman to Nathaniel Bloom and John F.S. Gray, March 19–20, 1863, www.whitmanarchive.org.
101. Barrus, *Whitman and Burroughs*, 10.
102. Freedman, *William Douglas O'Connor*, 239.
103. Ellen M. O'Connor to Walt Whitman, November 20, 1870, www.whitmanarchive.org.
104. Calder, "Personal Recollections of Walt Whitman," 828.
105. Ibid., 826–27.
106. Ibid., 828.
107. Barrus, *Whitman and Burroughs*, 6, 18.
108. Ibid., 7.
109. Ibid., 13.
110. Ibid., 17.
111. Ibid., 16.
112. Epstein, *Lincoln and Whitman*, 10–11.
113. Whitman, "Washington in the Hot Season."
114. Whitman, *Memoranda*, 39–41.
115. O'Connor, *Good Gray Poet*, 5.
116. Burlingame and Ettlinger, *Inside Lincoln's White House*, 102.
117. Grier, *Notebooks and Unpublished Prose Manuscripts*, 539.

CHAPTER 6

118. Walt Whitman to Lewis K. Brown, November 8–9, 1863, www.whitmanarchive.org.
119. Grier, *Notebooks and Unpublished Prose Manuscripts*, 659–61.

120. Trowbridge, *My Own Story*, 377–78.
121. Ibid., 388–89.
122. Whitman, *Memoranda*, 52.
123. Walt Whitman to Louisa Van Velsor Whitman, April 26, 1864, www. whitmanarchive.org.
124. Calder, "Personal Recollections of Walt Whitman," 833.
125. Johnson and Johnson, *In the Shadow of the United States Capitol*, 96–99.
126. Grier, *Notebooks and Unpublished Prose Manuscripts*, 680–81.
127. Murray, "Traveling with the Wounded."
128. Helen S. Cunningham to Walt Whitman, May 9 and June 11, 1864, www.whitmanarchive.org.
129. Murray, "Pete the Great," www.whitmanarchive.org.
130. Grier, *Notebooks and Unpublished Prose Manuscripts*, 549.
131. Calder, "Personal Recollections of Walt Whitman," 833.
132. Walt Whitman to Louisa Van Velsor Whitman, May 25, 1864, www. whitmanarchive.org.
133. Ibid., May 18 and May 30, 1864, www.whitmanarchive.org.
134. Ibid., June 3, 1864, www.whitmanarchive.org.
135. Ibid., June 7, 1864, www.whitmanarchive.org.
136. Ibid., June 17, 1864, www.whitmanarchive.org.
137. John Burroughs to Walt Whitman, August 2, 1864, www. whitmanarchive.org.
138. Whitman, "Our Wounded and Sick Soldiers."

Chapter 7

139. Epstein, *Lincoln and Whitman*, 136.
140. Walt Whitman to Thomas P. Sawyer, April 26, 1863, www. whitmanarchive.org.
141. Alonzo S. Bush to Walt Whitman, December 22, 1863, www. whitmanarchive.org.
142. Biographical information about Peter Doyle is from Murray, "Pete the Great."
143. Bucke, *Calamus*, 23.
144. Murray, "Pete the Great."
145. Bucke, *Calamus*, 24.
146. Ibid., 24–25.

147. Traubel, *With Walt Whitman in Camden*, 2:511.
148. Bucke, *Calamus*, 26–27.
149. Ibid., 31.
150. Ibid., 30.
151. Ibid., 28.
152. Ibid., 28.
153. Ibid., 29.
154. Ibid., 25.
155. Ibid., September 25, 1868, in Bucke, *Calamus*, 36.
156. Ibid., October 18, 1868, in Bucke, *Calamus*, 49.
157. Ibid., August 21, 1869, in Bucke, *Calamus*, 53–55.
158. Ibid., September 3, 1869, in Bucke, *Calamus*, 56.
159. Ibid., August 22, 1870, in Bucke, *Calamus*, 68.
160. Ibid., 27.
161. Grier, *Notebooks and Unpublished Prose Manuscripts*, 887–89.
162. Walt Whitman to Peter Doyle, July 30, 1870, in Bucke, *Calamus*, 61.
163. Ibid., September 6, 1870, in Bucke, *Calamus*, 73.

CHAPTER 8

164. Whitman, *Memoranda*, 74.
165. Whitman, "Last Hours of Congress."
166. Ibid.
167. Ibid.
168. Ibid.
169. Whitman, "Washington."
170. *Evening Star*, "Inauguration Ball."
171. Ibid., "Lieut. Gen'l Grant."
172. Bucke, *Calamus*, 25–26.
173. *Evening Star*, "Assassination of the President."
174. Whitman, *Memoranda*, 115.
175. Grier, *Notebooks and Unpublished Prose Manuscripts*, 2:763.
176. Whitman, *Specimen Days*, 763–64.
177. Morris, *Better Angel*, 228.
178. Traubel, *With Walt Whitman in Camden*, 2:304.
179. Burroughs, *Notes on Walt Whitman*, 101.

Chapter 9

180. William D. O'Connor to Walt Whitman, December 30, 1864, www. whitmanarchive.org

181. Walt Whitman to William D. O'Connor, January 6, 1865, www. whitmanarchive.org

182. Walt Whitman to Thomas Jefferson Whitman, January 30, 1865, www. whitmanarchive.org

183. Whitman, *November Boughs*, in *Walt Whitman: Poetry and Prose*, 1,171–72.

184. George Washington Whitman to Louisa Van Velsor Whitman, October 2 and October 23, 1864, in Loving, *Civil War Letters of George Washington Whitman*, 132–33.

185. Whitman, "Fifty-First New York City Veterans."

186. Grier, *Notebooks and Unpublished Prose Manuscripts*, 744–45.

187. Whitman, "Our Prisoners"; ibid., "Prisoners."

188. Thomas Jefferson Whitman to Walt Whitman, January 31, 1865, www. whitmanarchive.org.

189. George Washington Whitman to Louisa Van Velsor Whitman, February 24, 1865, in Loving, *Civil War Letters of George Washington Whitman*, 134.

190. Grier, *Notebooks and Unpublished Prose Manuscripts*, 716.

191. George Washington Whitman to Walt Whitman, July 14, 1865, in Loving, *Civil War Letters of George Washington Whitman*, 136.

192. Grier, *Notebooks and Unpublished Prose Manuscripts*, 2:756.

193. George Washington Whitman to Louisa Van Velsor Whitman, May 8, 1865, in Loving, *Civil War Letters of George Washington Whitman*, 135.

194. Whitman, *Memoranda*, 93.

195. Ibid., 93–94.

196. Ibid., 97.

197. Grier, *Notebooks and Unpublished Prose Manuscripts*, 756.

198. Whitman, *Memoranda*, 106.

199. Ibid., 82.

200. Walt Whitman to Alfred Pratt, July 25, 1867, www.whitmanarchive.org.

201. Walt Whitman to Anson Ryder Jr., August 15–16, 1865, www. whitmanarchive.org.

202. Ibid., September 27, 1866, www.whitmanarchive.org.

203. Grier, *Notebooks and Unpublished Prose Manuscripts*, 2:851.

204. Bucke, *Calamus*, 30.

205. James, "Mr. Walt Whitman."

206. Howells, "Drum-Taps."

207. Burroughs, "Walt Whitman and His 'Drum Taps.'"
208. Traubel, *With Walt Whitman in Camden*, 3:541–42.

CHAPTER 10

209. Hinton, "Washington Letter."
210. Traubel, *With Walt Whitman in Camden*, 1:148.
211. Freedman, *William Douglas O'Connor*, 158–60.
212. O'Connor, *Good Gray Poet*, 6.
213. Grier, *Notebooks and Unpublished Prose Manuscripts*, 798.
214. James Harlan to Walt Whitman, June 30, 1865, www.whitmanarchive.org.
215. Barrus, *Whitman and Burroughs*, 26.
216. Grier, *Notebooks and Unpublished Prose Manuscripts*, 799.
217. Barrus, *Whitman and Burroughs*, 27–30.
218. Mencken, *Prejudices*, 149.
219. O'Connor, *Good Gray Poet*, 34.
220. Freedman, *William Douglas O'Connor*, 178.
221. Barrus, *Whitman and Burroughs*, 261–62.
222. Walt Whitman to John Burroughs, July 2, 1866, www.whitmanarchiveorg.
223. Ibid. to Alfred Pratt, August 26, 1865, www.whitmanarchive.org.
224. Ibid.to Louisa Van Velsor Whitman, April 28–May 4, 1868, www.whitmanarchive.org.
225. Ibid. to Moncure D. Conway, February 17, 1868, www.whitmanarchive.org.
226. Ibid.to Louisa Van Velsor Whitman, December 28–29, 1871, www.whitmanarchive.org.
227. *Evening Star*, "Washington News and Gossip"; Murray, "Walt Whitman Laughs."

CHAPTER 11

228. Harold Bloom, "Afterthought," in Bloom, *Walt Whitman*, 231.
229. William Douglas O'Connor to Walt Whitman, August 13, 1864, www.whitmanarchive.org.
230. Walt Whitman to Thomas Jefferson Whitman, May 7, 1864, www.whitmanarchive.org.

231. Grant, *Personal Memoirs of U.S. Grant*, 373–74.

232. Walt Whitman to Louisa Van Velsor Whitman, June 10 1864, www.whitmanarchive.org.

233. Traubel, *With Walt Whitman in Camden*, 8:554.

234. Barrus, *Whitman and Burroughs*, 351.

235. Calder, "Personal Recollections of Walt Whitman," 831.

236. Freedman, *William Douglas O'Connor*, 255.

237. Eldridge, "Walt Whitman as a Conservative."

238. Calder, "Personal Recollections of Walt Whitman," 827.

239. Barrus, *Whitman and Burroughs*, 20.

240. Calder, "Personal Recollections of Walt Whitman," 827.

241. Burroughs, *Notes on Walt Whitman*, 85–86.

242. *Evening Star*, "Department Clerks and Their Official Heads."

243. Walt Whitman, *Democratic Vistas*, in *Walt Whitman: Poetry and Prose*, 937.

244. Ibid., 937–38.

245. Ibid., 935.

246. Ibid., 933.

247. Ibid., 961.

248. *Evening Star*, "Telegrams to the Star."

249. Murray, "Whitman Takes on D.C.'s Dailies," 52.

250. Bucke, *Calamus*, 32.

251. Murray, "Whitman Takes on D.C.'s Dailies," 47–57; ibid., "Pete the Great."

252. *Evening Star*, "Policeman Who Arrested a Sleeping Infant."

253. Grier, *Notebooks and Unpublished Prose Manuscripts*, 783.

254. *Evening Star*, "Policeman Tried and Cleared."

255. *Critic-Record*, December 30, 1871, and *Evening Star*, "A Police Officer Killed by a Woman," December 30, 1871.

256. *Evening Star*, "Funeral of the Late Policeman Doyle," January 1, 1872.

257. Walt Whitman to Louisa Van Velsor Whitman, January 1, 1872, www.whitmanarchive.org.

258. *Evening Star*, "Trial of a Woman for Murder," April 4, 1872, and *Evening Star*, "Trial of Mrs. Shea for the Murder of Police Officer Doyle," April 5, 1872.

259. Griswold and Stoddard, eds., *Poets and Poetry of America*, 626–27.

260. *Evening Star*, October 3, 1871.

261. *Evening Star*, "'Reliably Dead,'" April 8, 1871.

262. *New York Herald*, "Dartmouth College," June 27, 1872.

263. *Evening Star*, "Walt Whitman's Poem To-day at Dartmouth College," June 26, 1872.

264. *New York Times*, Charles Eldridge, "Walt Whitman as a Conservative," June 7, 1902.

265. Whitman, *Democratic Vistas*, 930.

266. Barrus, *Comrades*, 96.

267. Freedman, *William Douglas O'Connor*, 256.

268. Barrus, *Comrades*, 80.

Chapter 12

269. Bucke, *Calamus*, iii.

270. Ibid., 31.

271. Barrus, *Comrades*, 81.

272. *Notebooks and Unpublished Prose Manuscripts*, 2:917–919.

273. Barrus, *Comrades*, 83.

274. Walt Whitman to Peter Doyle, June 26, 1873, in Bucke, *Calamus*, 101.

275. Walt Whitman to Peter Doyle, July 24, 1873, in Bucke, *Calamus*, 104.

276. Walt Whitman to Ellen M. O'Connor, June 10, 1874, www. whitmanarchive.org.

277. Bucke, *Calamus*, 25.

278. Whitman, *Complete Prose Works*, 513.

279. Murray, "Pete the Great."

280. Bucke, *Calamus*, 32–33.

281. Murray, "Pete the Great."

BIBLIOGRAPHY

BOOKS

Alcott, Louisa May. *Hospital Sketches*. Edited by Elaine Showalter. *Alternative Alcott*. New Brunswick: Rutgers University Press, 1988.

Ames, Mary Clemmer. *Ten Years in Washington*. Hartford, CT: A.D. Worthington & Co, 1873.

Barrus, Clara. *Whitman and Burroughs: Comrades*. Boston: Houghton Mifflin, 1931.

Bloom, Harold, ed. *Walt Whitman*. New York: Chelsea House, 2006.

Brown, George Rothwell. *Washington: A Not Too Serious History*. Baltimore, MD: Norman Publishing, 1930.

Bucke, Richard Maurice, ed. *Calamus: A Series of Letters Written During the Years 1868–1880 by Walt Whitman to a Young Friend (Peter Doyle)*. Boston: Laurens Maynard, 1897.

Burlingame, Michael, and John R. Turner Ettlinger, eds. *Inside Lincoln's White House: The Complete Civil War Diary of John Hay*. Carbondale: Southern Illinois University Press, 1997.

Burroughs, John. *Notes on Walt Whitman as Poet and Person*. 2nd edition. New York: J.S. Redfield, 1872.

Dickens, Charles. *American Notes and Pictures from Italy*. 1842. New York: Scribner, 1898.

Epstein, Daniel Mark. *Lincoln and Whitman: Parallel Lives in Civil War Washington.* New York: Ballantine Books, 2004.

Freedman, Florence Bernstein. *William Douglas O'Connor: Walt Whitman's Chosen Knight.* Athens: Ohio University Press, 1985.

Genoways, Ted. *Walt Whitman and the Civil War: America's Poet During the Lost Years of 1860–1862.* Berkeley: University of California Press, 2009.

Grant, Ulysses S. *Personal Memoirs of U.S. Grant.* New York: Da Capo Press, 1983.

Grier, Edward F., ed. *Walt Whitman: Notebooks and Unpublished Prose Manuscripts.* Vol. 2. New York: New York University Press, 1984.

Griswold, Rufus Wilmot, and Richard Henry Stoddard, eds. *The Poets and Poetry of America.* New York: James Miller, 1872.

Hawthorne, Nathaniel. "Chiefly About War Matters." In *Sketches and Studies.* Boston: Houghton Mifflin, 1862.

Howells, William Dean. *Literary Friends and Acquaintances: A Personal Retrospect of American Authorship.* New York: Harper & Brothers, 1900.

Janke, Lucinda Prout. *A Guide to Civil War Washington, D.C.: The Capital of the Union.* Charleston, SC: The History Press, 2013.

Johnson, Abby A., and Ronald M. Johnson. *In the Shadow of the United States Capitol: Congressional Cemetery and the Memory of the Nation.* Washington, D.C.: New Academia Publishing, 2012.

Kaplan, Justin. *Walt Whitman: A Life.* New York: Harper Perennial Modern Classics, 2003.

Kummings, Donald D., ed. *A Companion to Walt Whitman.* Oxford, UK: Blackwell, 2006.

Leech, Margaret. *Reveille in Washington: 1860–1865.* New York: New York Review Books Classics, 2011.

LeMaster, J.R., and Donald D. Kummings, eds. *The Routledge Encyclopedia of Walt Whitman.* New York: Routledge, 1998.

Loving, Jerome M., ed. *Civil War Letters of George Washington Whitman.* Durham, NC: Duke University Press, 1975.

———. *Walt Whitman: The Song of Himself.* Berkeley: University of California Press, 1999.

Martin, Justin. *Rebel Souls: Walt Whitman and America's First Bohemians.* Boston: Da Capo Press, 2014.

Mencken, H.L. *Prejudices: First, Second, and Third Series.* New York: Penguin/ Library of America, 2010.

Morris, Roy, Jr. *The Better Angel: Walt Whitman in the Civil War.* New York: Oxford University Press, 2000.

BIBLIOGRAPHY

Myerson, Joel, and Daniel Shealy, eds. *The Journals of Louisa May Alcott.* Boston: Little, Brown and Company, 1989.

Oates, Stephen B. *A Woman of Valor: Clara Barton and the Civil War.* New York: Free Press, 1994.

O'Connor, William Douglas. *The Good Gray Poet: A Vindication.* New York: Bunce & Huntington, 1866.

Reynolds, David S. *Walt Whitman's America: A Cultural Biography.* New York: Random House, 1995.

Rhodes, Elisha Hunt. *All for the Union: The Civil War Diary and Letters of Elisha Hunt Rhodes.* New York: Orion Books, 1985.

Robertson, Michael. *Worshipping Walt: The Whitman Disciples.* Princeton, NJ: Princeton University Press, 2008.

Roper, Robert. *Now the Drum of War: Walt Whitman and His Brothers in the Civil War.* New York: Walker & Company, 2008.

Stearns, Amanda Akin. *The Lady Nurse of Ward E.* New York: Baker & Taylor, 1909.

Swanson, James L. *Manhunt: The Twelve-Day Chase for Lincoln's Killer.* New York: Harper Perennial, 2006.

Traubel, Horace. *With Walt Whitman in Camden.* Vol. 1. Boston: Small, Maynard, 1906.

———. *With Walt Whitman in Camden.* Vol. 2. New York: Mitchell Kennerley, 1915.

———. *With Walt Whitman in Camden.* Vol. 3. New York: Mitchell Kennerley, 1914.

———. *With Walt Whitman in Camden.* Vol. 8. Edited by Jeanne Chapman and Robert MacIsaac. Oregon House, CA: W.L. Bentley, 1996.

Trollope, Anthony. *North America.* New York: Harpers, 1862.

Trowbridge, John Townsend. *My Own Story with Recollections of Noted Persons.* Boston: Houghton Mifflin, 1903.

Walt Whitman: Poetry and Prose. New York: Penguin/Library of America, 1982.

Whitman, Walt. *Complete Prose Works.* New York: D. Appleton, 1910.

———. *Memoranda During the War.* Edited by Peter Coviello. New York: Oxford University Press, 2004.

Winkle, Kenneth J. *Lincoln's Citadel: The Civil War in Washington, DC.* New York: W.W. Norton, 2013.

COLLECTIONS

Historical Society of Washington, D.C.
Manuscript Division, Library of Congress, Washington, D.C.
National Museum of Civil War Medicine, Frederick, MD.
Prints & Photographs Division, Library of Congress, Washington, D.C.
Walt Whitman Archive, www.whitmanarchive.org.

JOURNALS

Murray, Martin G. "'By Broad Potomac Shore': Walt Whitman & Congressional Cemetery." *Heritage Gazette*, Summer 2005.

———. "Pete the Great: A Biography of Peter Doyle." *Walt Whitman Quarterly Review* 12, no. 1 (Summer 1994): 1–51.

———. "Traveling with the Wounded: Walt Whitman and Washington's Civil War Hospitals." *Washington History: Magazine of the Historical Society of Washington, D.C.* 8 (Fall/Winter 1996–97): 58–73, 92–93.

———. "Walt Whitman Laughs: An Uncollected Piece of Prose Journalism." *Walt Whitman Quarterly Review* 30 (2013): 138–49.

———. "Whitman Takes on D.C.'s Dailies," *Yale University Library Gazette* 70, nos. 1–2 (October 1995): 47–57.

Roberts, Kim. "A Map of Whitman's Washington Boarding Houses and Work Places." *Walt Whitman Quarterly Review* 22 (Summer 2004): 23–28.

NEWSPAPERS & PERIODICALS

Burroughs, John. "Walt Whitman and His 'Drum Taps'." *Galaxy*, December 1, 1866, 606–15.

Calder, Ellen M. Tarr O'Connor. "Personal Recollections of Walt Whitman." *Atlantic Monthly*, June 1907, 825–34.

Critic-Record, July 11, 1871; December 30, 1871.

Eldridge, Charles. "Walt Whitman as a Conservative." *New York Times*, June 7, 1902.

Evening Star. "Assassination of the President." April 15, 1865.

———. "Department Clerks and Their Official Heads." September 9, 1868.

———. "Funeral of the Late Policeman Doyle." January 1, 1872.

———. "The Inauguration Ball." March 7, 1865.

———. "Lieut. Gen'l Grant." April 14, 1865.

———. October 3, 1871.

———. "Policeman Tried and Cleared." July 8, 1871.

———. "The Policeman Who Arrested a Sleeping Infant." May 18, 1871.

———. "A Police Officer Killed by a Woman." December 30, 1871.

———. "'Reliably Dead.'" April 8, 1871.

———. "Telegrams to the Star." September 7, 1871.

———. "Trial of a Woman for Murder." April 4, 1872.

———. "Trial of Mrs. Shea for the Murder of Police Officer Doyle." April 5, 1872.

———. "Walt Whitman's Poem To-day at Dartmouth College." June 26, 1872.

———. "Washington News and Gossip." October 17, 1872.

Hay, John. "From Washington (From Our Special Correspondent)." *New York World*, March 4, 1861.

Hinton, Richard. "Washington Letter," *Cincinnati Commercial*, August 26, 1871.

Howells, William Dean. "Drum-Taps." *Round Table*, November 11, 1865, 147–48.

James, Henry. "Mr. Walt Whitman." *The Nation*, November 16, 1865, 625–26.

New York Herald. "Dartmouth College." June 27, 1872.

Swinton, John. "Walt Whitman." *New York Herald*, April 1, 1876.

Whitman, Walt. "Fifty-First New York City Veterans." *New York Times*, October 29, 1864.

———. "The Great Army of the Sick." *New York Times*, February 26, 1863.

———. "The Great Washington Hospitals: Life Among Fifty Thousand Soldiers." *Brooklyn Daily Eagle*, March 19, 1863.

———. "The Last Hours of Congress." *New York Times*, March 6, 1865.

———. "Our National City." *New York Times*, October 4, 1863.

———. "Our Prisoners." *Brooklyn Daily Eagle*, December 27, 1864.

———. "Our Wounded and Sick Soldiers." *New York Times*, December 11, 1864.

———. "The Prisoners." *New York Times*, December 27, 1864.

———. "Washington." *New York Times*, March 12, 1865.

———. "Washington in the Hot Season." *New York Times*, August 16, 1863.

RECORDS

Boyd's Washington Directory. Various years, 1861 to 1875.

INDEX